# UTAH & NEVADA
## 50 HIKES WITH KIDS

# UTAH &
# NEVADA
# 50 HIKES
# WITH KIDS

## WENDY GORTON
## AND HAILEY TERRY

Timber Press · Portland, Oregon

Frontispiece: Kirk tackles a canyon.

Published in 2023 by Timber Press, Inc.,
a subsidiary of Workman Publishing Co., Inc.,
a subsidiary of Hachette Book Group, Inc.
1290 Avenue of the Americas
New York, New York 10104

timberpress.com

Printed in China on responsibly sourced paper

Series design by Hillary Caudle; layout by Sarah Crumb
Cover design and illustration by Always With Honor
Inside cover map by Nick Trotter

The publisher is not responsible for websites (or their content)
that are not owned by the publisher.

The Hachette Speakers Bureau provides a wide range of authors for
speaking events. To find out more, go to HachetteSpeakersBureau.com
or email HachetteSpeakers@hbgusa.com.

ISBN 978-1-64326-155-3

A catalog record for this book is also available from the British Library.

To Larry, whose patience and calmness set such a great example for our youngest adventurers as we made it through the inevitable bumps of the journey.
—Wendy

To my sweet boy, Kirk, who made me a mother and was there every step of the way as I rediscovered myself on the trail as a new mom.
—Hailey

# CONTENTS

------------------------------------

## ADVENTURES IN
## UTAH

## ADVENTURES IN
## NEVADA

------------------------------------

# PREFACE

Utah and Nevada are two of the most diverse states when it comes to outdoor adventure. One day you're in Salt Lake City, hiking through the snowy evergreen-covered mountains, and the next you're three hours south in Moab, scrambling over red rock and checking out all the desert life that's around you. Utah is home to the Great Salt Lake, the largest saltwater lake in the Western Hemisphere; Delicate Arch, a 52-foot-tall freestanding natural arch that has been proclaimed the world's most famous arch; the Cottonwood Canyons, one of the snowiest places in the world, averaging 551 inches of snow a year; and Bryce Canyon, containing the largest number of hoodoos (geologic spires) in the world. Nevada is covered by the Basin and Range region, boasting more than 150 mountain ranges, some of which you'll drive and hike through at Great Basin National Park and beyond. Nevada produces three-quarters of the gold mined in the United States, and is full of mining and railroad historical sites, like Ward Charcoal Ovens and Rhyolite Ghost Town. You'll also explore unique geological formations at Cathedral Gorge, Red Rock Canyon, and the Valley of Fire. Almost 60 percent of these states are public lands, so Utah and Nevada are open and perfect for taking your children exploring.

Hailey grew up in Las Vegas, Nevada, and Utah has been her home since she moved there for college. She's spent years exploring the outdoor world here but feels like she's barely scratched the surface. The region offers rock climbing, backpacking, fly fishing, paddleboarding, mountain biking, skiing, and so many other sports—it really is the perfect place to try a new hobby outside. Hailey even had her first baby right here in Salt Lake City and hiked with him through the freezing winter. She got a carrier for Kirk to ride in, and together they racked up a lot of miles.

Smack in the middle of her second year of teaching fourth graders, Wendy became a PolarTREC GoNorth! teacher-explorer. She packed up with a top-notch, experienced adventure crew and set out to spend two weeks dogsledding, interviewing locals about climate change, and collecting snowpack data. It was the hardest thing she'd ever done to date, but it introduced her to adventure learning pioneered by the University of Minnesota's Dr. Aaron Doering. Wendy's goal was to help interpret the experience for her students back in her classroom and students from around the world who wanted to feel a piece of real-life adventure. Every night, the dogs rushed them through the snow to the next research hut in the middle of Finland. Once inside, they peeled off their layers, cooked dinner from meal rations, used maps to plan the next day, and got a good night's sleep. Wendy was physically and mentally exhausted, but she still managed to take pictures, create activities, and even host a live webinar with her home classroom.

Then as now, she studied each day's route with the eyes of a child—finding the nooks that delighted her, asking herself big questions, documenting things that interested her but that she couldn't identify on the spot, and researching answers. Fourteen years later, Wendy is thrilled to be creating mini-adventures in Utah and Nevada for families, helping them become their own intrepid adventurers. Her father began exploring Utah's remote wilderness as a teenager and brought Wendy and her sister as toddlers, so its red rocks have been a part of her life and outdoor inspiration for a long time. She and her family make it out to the Southwest several times a year, exploring new slot canyons and small towns. Her interest in helping raise a generation of resilient, curious kids also extends to her day job in education, a field she chose because she wants to make sure every child gets a chance to fall in love with a subject that resonates and to make it his or her life's work.

The driving question behind this book is how we can design experiences that inspire wonder in our children. That is the question to keep in mind as you use this book too. If we can provide a fun environment and the initial sparks of curiosity, we can—as educators, caregivers, aunties and uncles, grandparents, and parents—help children discover and explore the world around them and learn to appreciate natural beauty even from the youngest of ages. The aim of this guide is to give adults some tools to help ignite questions on the trail, to teach kids that it's great to stop and look at things instead of just rushing from point A to point B, and to begin to introduce a broader understanding of just how many unique places you live near in this region. By simply venturing out and interacting with kids along the trail, we are building the skills they need to learn how to question things they see around them—everywhere—and to look for answers.

Many of these adventures provide a taste of treks kids may embark on as teenagers or adults—imagine them summiting 13,065-foot Wheeler Peak in Great Basin National Park in a few years. In the meantime, this guide aims to provide kids of all ages a curated selection of some of the most varied and interesting destinations in Utah and Nevada while reassuring busy adults about what exactly to expect from any given trail, the features they will see when they arrive, and the logistics that can make or break an outdoor excursion with kids. We hope you get a sense of the love steeped in these pages—the love for outdoors, the love for adventure, the love for planning and preparation, and the love for family and community. Our family members were co-adventurers on every hike, tackling bathroom mishaps, downed trees, and often squeezing in as many as four hikes a day to test and find just the right ones for this guide—choosing which adventures to include was no easy task. The region's number of kid-friendly hikes is almost staggering, but we developed a firm kid filter of awesome features: simple driving and turnkey instructions on the trail so you're not second-guessing yourselves, honest-to-goodness dirt on the bottom of your shoes and not pavement, and no interpretive signs, giving you a more adventurous and hike-like experience rather than a sterile stroll.

Many of us have seen the copious amounts of research about the benefits of getting kids outdoors more and interacting with the world in an open-ended way. As you romp with your own crew through the outdoors, keep in mind that while the scavenger hunt items called out on each hike might help you add excitement or teachable moments, finding them all

Bringing a special toy can make hikes that much more special to your kids. (Kirk loves to bring his cars!)

should not be the main goal of your outing. We wrote this guide to help you get outside, spend time with your family, and have fun.

Peter Gray, a Boston College research professor and expert on children's play, encourages parents to include other kids on adventures. "When you go on a hike or a trip, think about inviting other families or joining group hikes. Kids need other kids. This frees you, the adult, as well as your child, so you can interact with other adults. They can go ahead safely on the trail, and you don't have to go and amuse them because they are learning and playing with their peers. Don't try to cover too much ground—stop and let them play wherever they are."

Kids lead more structured lives today than ever before in history. We think you'll be pleasantly surprised when you see how much they enjoy simply being set loose in wide-open spaces. We hope this guide will help you foster curiosity and a love of nature in the kids in your lives and that it helps to raise our next generation of naturalists by putting the guidebook in their hands. Experiencing the wonders all around us creates lifelong habits of seeking out adventure, appreciating the gifts nature gives us every day, and caring about keeping our natural resources clean, beautiful, and accessible for many future generations. All the scaffolds you'll need to plan even more of your own adventures are here.

# CHOOSING YOUR ADVENTURE

Your little adventurer might one day proclaim "Let's canyoneer!" This guide is designed to help children become co-adventurers with you across the diverse Utah and Nevada landscape, exploring some of the most incredible canyons on the planet. Build excitement by involving them in the planning process from the beginning. Let them flip through and mark the pages they'd like to tackle in the future. Ask them what features they love when they're outside. How hard do they feel like working today for their adventure? How long do they want to hike? You'll find the closest town as well as the closest adventure hub, the larger cities of the region. For maximum success with younger kids, no hike is over 5 miles long or gains more than 1200 feet—perfectly attainable for most little legs. This means that there can be plenty of time for exploration, rest stops, snacks, and just taking in the sights and sounds around you. Challenging means it's going to be a little bit of work for young legs, but it won't be an adult level of challenging.

# ADVENTURES IN
# UTAH

| ADVENTURE | HUB | LENGTH (MILES) | DIFFICULTY/ ELEVATION | HIGHLIGHTS |
|---|---|---|---|---|
| **1** Limber Pine Nature Trail *PAGE 60* | Bear Lake | 1.5 | Moderate 174' | Large limber pine |
| **2** Icebox Canyon *PAGE 64* | Ogden/ Pineview Reservoir | 3.4 | Challenging 535' | Canyon, creek |
| **3** Buffalo Point *PAGE 68* | Antelope Island | 1.2 | Moderate 285' | View of Great Salt Lake, rocks to climb on, buffalo sightings |
| **4** Wild Rose Trail *PAGE 72* | Salt Lake City | 2 | Moderate 354' | Wildflowers |
| **5** Bear Canyon Suspension Bridge *PAGE 76* | Draper | 2.1 | Challenging 436' | Bridge, view of Salt Lake County |
| **6** Donut Falls *PAGE 80* | Salt Lake City | 1.5 | Moderate 308' | Waterfall, wildflowers, river crossings |
| **7** Stewart Falls *PAGE 84* | Provo/ Sundance Resort | 3.8 | Challenging 282' | Waterfall, lots of greenery, wildlife |
| **8** Maple Canyon Arch *PAGE 88* | Fountain Green | 1.7 | Moderate 551' | Arch, rock climbers, conglomerate rock |

| ADVENTURE | HUB | LENGTH (MILES) | DIFFICULTY/ ELEVATION | HIGHLIGHTS |
|---|---|---|---|---|
| **9** Fifth Water Hot Springs *PAGE 92* | Spanish Fork | 4.7 | Challenging 607' | Hot springs, river, plant life |
| **10** Mirror Lake *PAGE 96* | Kamas | 1.6 | Easy 39' | Lake, fishing, wildlife |
| **11** Red Fleet State Park *PAGE 100* | Vernal | 2 | Challenging 272' | Reservoir, geological formations, dinosaur tracks |
| **12** Landscape Arch *PAGE 104* | Moab | 2.4 | Easy 308' | Three arches, geology |
| **13** Turret Arch and the Windows *PAGE 108* | Moab | 1.8 | Easy 282' | Two arches and two windows, views, geology |
| **14** Whale Rock *PAGE 112* | Moab | 1 | Moderate 112' | Summit, geological formations |
| **15** Grand View Point *PAGE 116* | Moab | 1.9 | Moderate 197' | Views, geology |
| **16** Hovenweep Ruins *PAGE 120* | Blanding | 1.8 | Easy 141' | Ravine, historic ruins |
| **17** Butler Wash Ruins *PAGE 124* | Blanding | 1 | Easy 108' | Geology, historic ruins |
| **18** Sipapu Natural Bridge *PAGE 128* | Blanding | 1.3 | Challenging 404' | Natural bridge, ladder climbs |

| ADVENTURE | HUB | LENGTH (MILES) | DIFFICULTY/ ELEVATION | HIGHLIGHTS |
|---|---|---|---|---|
| 19 Goblin Valley PAGE 132 | Hanksville | 1 | Easy 69' | Geological formations |
| 20 Hickman Natural Bridge PAGE 136 | Torrey | 1.9 | Moderate 449' | Natural bridges, views, geology |
| 21 Sunset Point PAGE 140 | Torrey | 0.9 | Easy 33' | Views, geology |
| 22 Devil's Garden PAGE 144 | Escalante | 0.8 | Easy 92' | Geological formations |
| 23 Lower Calf Creek Falls PAGE 148 | Escalante | 6.4 | Challenging 820' | Waterfall, creek, cool trees/colors |
| 24 Panorama Point PAGE 152 | Cannonville/ Tropic | 3.2 | Moderate 292' | Unique geological spires and cave |
| 25 Queens Garden PAGE 156 | Bryce/Tropic | 2.1 | Moderate 453' | Views, hoodoos |
| 26 Bristlecone Pine Loop PAGE 160 | Bryce/Tropic | 1.1 | Easy 118' | Views, bristlecone pines |
| 27 Red Hollow Slot Canyon PAGE 164 | Orderville | 1.1 | Moderate 207' | Slot canyon |

| ADVENTURE | HUB | LENGTH (MILES) | DIFFICULTY/ ELEVATION | HIGHLIGHTS |
|---|---|---|---|---|
| 28 Kanab Sand Caves PAGE 168 | Kanab | 0.8 | Challenging 157' | Sand caves, views |
| 29 Coral Pink Sand Dunes PAGE 172 | Kanab | 1 | Moderate 59' | Pink sand dunes |
| 30 Toadstools PAGE 176 | Kanab | 2 | Easy 125' | Cool hoodoos |
| 31 Cascade Falls PAGE 180 | Duck Creek Village/ Navajo Lake | 1.2 | Moderate 125' | Waterfall, views, huge trees |
| 32 Hidden Haven Falls PAGE 184 | Brian Head | 1.4 | Challenging 275' | Waterfall, lots of scrambling, wildflowers |
| 33 Timber Creek Overlook PAGE 188 | Springdale | 1.2 | Moderate 269' | View of Zion |
| 34 Watchman PAGE 192 | Springdale | 3.2 | Challenging 640' | Views, geology |
| 35 Zion Canyon Overlook PAGE 196 | Springdale | 1 | Moderate 430' | Boardwalk, views, geology |
| 36 Lava Tubes Trail PAGE 200 | St. George/ Snow Canyon State Park | 1.4 | Moderate 184' | Spelunking, desert plants |

# ADVENTURES IN
# NEVADA

| ADVENTURE | HUB | LENGTH (MILES) | DIFFICULTY/ ELEVATION | HIGHLIGHTS |
|---|---|---|---|---|
| **37** White Domes *PAGE 206* | Las Vegas | 1.2 | Moderate 328' | Amazing white domes and red rock geology |
| **38** Mouse's Tank *PAGE 210* | Las Vegas | 0.9 | Easy 56' | Petroglyphs, history |
| **39** Railroad Tunnel *PAGE 214* | Boulder City/ Hoover Dam | 3 | Easy 29' | Tunnels, view of Lake Mead, bighorn sheep |
| **40** Calico Tanks *PAGE 218* | Las Vegas/ Red Rock Canyon National Conservation Area | 2.7 | Challenging 427' | Rocks to climb on, water tanks, view of Red Rock Canyon |
| **41** Moon Caves *PAGE 222* | Pioche/ Las Vegas | 0.9 | Challenging 30' | Slot canyon, history |
| **42** Alpine Lakes *PAGE 226* | Baker | 2.7 | Challenging 472' | Views, lakes |

| ADVENTURE | HUB | LENGTH (MILES) | DIFFICULTY/ ELEVATION | HIGHLIGHTS |
|---|---|---|---|---|
| **43** Ward Charcoal Ovens State Park PAGE 230 | Ely | 1.1 | Easy 72' | Historic ovens, creek |
| **44** Smith Lake PAGE 234 | Wells | 2.5 | Challenging 790' | Views, lakes |
| **45** Griffith Canyon PAGE 238 | Reno | 1.4 | Moderate 164' | Petroglyphs, juniper trees |
| **46** Spooner Lake PAGE 242 | Carson City | 2.5 | Easy 135' | Lake, wildlife |
| **47** Fort Churchill PAGE 246 | Silver Springs | 1.6 | Easy 72' | Historic buildings, railroad, museum at trailhead |
| **48** Monkey Rock PAGE 250 | Carson City | 2.6 | Challenging 456' | View of Lake Tahoe, birds |
| **49** Rhyolite Ghost Town PAGE 254 | Beatty | 1.1 | Easy 118' | Historic buildings |
| **50** Mary Jane Falls PAGE 258 | Las Vegas | 3.9 | Challenging 1135' | Waterfall, fall foliage |

There are plenty
of lush forests
for you to explore
as well

# ADVENTURES BY
# FEATURE

Can you remember the first cave you explored? The first waterfall that
misted your face? Each of these adventures includes a destination or item
of particular interest to motivate young legs and reward hard work. Encourage kids, as co-adventurers, to talk about which types of natural features
tickle them the most and why.

| FEATURE | ADVENTURE |
|---|---|
| Lakes, ponds, and hot springs | (9) Fifth Water Hot Springs <br> (10) Mirror Lake <br> (40) Calico Tanks <br> (44) Smith Lake <br> (46) Spooner Lake |
| Waterfalls | (6) Donut Falls <br> (7) Stewart Falls <br> (23) Lower Calf Creek Falls <br> (31) Cascade Falls <br> (32) Hidden Haven Falls |
| History | (5) Bear Canyon Suspension Bridge <br> (16) Hovenweep Ruins <br> (17) Butler Wash Ruins <br> (39) Railroad Tunnel <br> (40) Calico Tanks <br> (43) Ward Charcoal Ovens State Park <br> (45) Petroglyphs at Griffith Canyon <br> (47) Fort Churchill |
| Flora and fauna | (4) Wildflowers at Wild Rose Trailhead <br> (6) Wildflowers at Donut Falls <br> (18) Gambel oak grove at the bottom of Sipapu Natural Bridge <br> (26) Bristlecone pine at Bristlecone Pine Loop <br> (32) Wildflowers at Hidden Haven Falls |

| FEATURE | ADVENTURE |
| --- | --- |
| Geology | **3** Buffalo Point |
| | **8** Maple Canyon Arch |
| | **9** Fifth Water Hot Springs |
| | **11** Dino tracks and ship buttes at Red Fleet State Park |
| | **12** Three arches at Landscape Arch |
| | **13** Windows at Turret Arch |
| | **14** Huge sandstone "whale" at Whale Rock |
| | **15** Island in the Sky view at Grand View Point |
| | **18** Sipapu Natural Bridge |
| | **19** Goblin rock structures at Goblin Valley |
| | **20** Hickman Natural Bridge |
| | **24** Spires at Panorama Point |
| | **29** Dunes at Coral Pink Sand Dunes |
| | **30** Toadstool formations at Toadstools |
| | **36** Lava Tubes |
| | **37** White Domes |
| | **41** Slot canyons at Cathedral Gorge |
| | **45** Petroglyphs at Griffith Canyon |
| | **48** Monkey Rock |

| FEATURE | ADVENTURE |
|---------|-----------|
| Caves | **11** Small cave at Red Fleet State Park |
| | **17** Cave at Butler Wash Ruins |
| | **24** Indian Cave at Panorama Point |
| | **28** Kanab Sand Caves |
| | **41** Caves at Cathedral Gorge State Park |
| Summits, peaks, and views | **3** Buffalo Point |
| | **15** View at Grand View Point |
| | **21** View at Sunset Point in Capitol Reef |
| | **25** View at Sunrise Point at Queens Garden |
| | **33** Timber Creek Overlook |
| | **34** View on top of the Watchman |
| | **35** Zion Canyon Overlook |
| | **40** Calico Tanks |
| | **48** Monkey Rock |
| River exploration | **2** Wheeler Creek at Icebox Canyon |
| | **6** Mill D South Fork Creek at Donut Falls |
| | **9** Fifth Water Hot Springs |
| | **31** Cascade Falls |
| | **43** Willow Creek at Ward Charcoal Ovens State Park |

| FEATURE | ADVENTURE |
|---|---|
| Campground by trailhead | **1** Sunrise at Limber Pine |
| | **2** Anderson Cove at Icebox Canyon |
| | **3** Bridger Bay at Buffalo Point |
| | **6** Jordan Pines near Donut Falls |
| | **7** Mount Timpanogos near Stewart Falls |
| | **8** Maple Canyon near Maple Canyon Arch |
| | **9** Fifth Water Hot Springs |
| | **10** Mirror Lake |
| | **11** Red Fleet State Park near the dinosaur tracks |
| | **12, 13** Devil's Garden near Landscape and Turret Arch |
| | **14, 15** Willow Flat or Dead Horse Point State Park near Whale Rock and Grand View Point |
| | **16** Hovenweep National Monument |
| | **17** Comb Wash near Butler Wash Ruins |
| | **18** Natural Bridges National Monument |
| | **19** Goblin Valley |
| | **20, 21** Fruita near Hickman Natural Bridge and Sunset Point |

| FEATURE | ADVENTURE |
|---------|-----------|
| Campground by trailhead, cont. | **22, 23** Calf Creek near Devils Garden and Lower Calf Creek Falls |
| | **24** Basin, Bryce View, and Arch at Kodachrome at Panorama Point |
| | **25, 26** Sunset and North at Bryce Canyon for Queens Garden and Bristlecone Pine Loop |
| | **29** Coral Pink Sand Dunes |
| | **34, 35** Watchman near the Watchman and Zion Canyon Overlook |
| | **36** Lava Tubes Trail |
| | **37** Atlatl by White Domes and Petroglyph Trail |
| | **40** Calico Tanks |
| | **41** Cathedral Gorge State Park |
| | **42** Alpine Lakes Loop Trail |
| | **43** Willow at Ward Charcoal Ovens State Park |
| | **44** Angel Lake at Smith Lake |
| | **47** Fort Churchill |

# ADVENTURES BY SEASON

Hiking builds character, so prepare your family to be ready for any season! You can also help kids appreciate the seasonal transformations by returning to a favorite hike in each season and asking "What has changed since our last visit?"

Fall is a favorite time for many families in Utah.

Many trails are available year-round for your adventuring pleasure, yet some really shine and sing during particular moments of the year. The spring is great for trails with waterfalls for maximum flow opportunities. Spring also brings a plethora of wildflowers, and using a guide like ours will help you and your kids begin to identify them. Hiking in spring can also bring muddy trail conditions—plan for proper footwear and consider a hiking stick.

Summer allows the best access to our higher elevation trails that might be snowed in during the winter and special, high-elevation wildflowers. Summer also is green and the perfect time for those water hikes—there's nothing quite like splashing in the river on a warm summer day. But summer also has copious flies and ticks, so bring repellent and always do checks.

The fall erupts with colorful foliage and mushrooms on many trails. There are so many bigtooth maple trees among the evergreen trees, and they pop as they change from green to yellow, orange, and red. However, hunting is also a popular fall activity at some trailheads—always check the signs and consider bringing orange shirts and hats in your adventure bag.

If the snow of winter isn't your thing, it's easy to escape it with a quick drive down south. There are miles of desert in Utah and Nevada that don't get snow and are actually best explored in the winter months! Winter also offers a great chance to visit many lower elevation trails. The snow and ice of winter, however, sometimes require snowshoes or spikes for your shoes. Call ahead to check on trail conditions.

If you want to get out year-round, one thing you'll have to learn quickly is that there is no such thing as bad weather, just bad clothes. The basics of layering for cold weather include the following:

- A non-cotton base layer
- A fleece mid layer (or similar)
- A waterproof outer layer

Hailey layered up her baby, added wool socks, a beanie, and face covering and hit the trails with snow all around them. Of course, she has her own winter gear that usually includes some layers, microspikes, hiking poles, mittens, and waterproof boots.

Southern Utah and southern Nevada can really beat you down in the summer. Hiking in the desert heat has its own challenges that you should be prepared for. Utah and Nevada are two of the driest states in the country, so drinking plenty of water is absolutely crucial. Adults should drink 1 liter of water for every 2 hours of hiking, and even more if it's a really hot, sunny day. Young kids need less, but still more than they would drink at home.

Sun coverage is also important when out in the sun—even in the winter! Wearing hats and sunscreen or UPF-rated clothing is a great way to protect skin. If you are hiking in the snow, it's still important to protect yourself because the sun will reflect off the snow and burn your exposed skin. All of the hikes are open in the summer, but in warmer areas you'll want to try to avoid midday heat and try hiking earlier or later in the evening.

| PEAK SEASON | ADVENTURE |
|---|---|
| Winter | **36** Lava Tubes |
| | **37, 38** White Domes and Mouse's Tank |
| | **40** Calico Tanks |
| | **47** Fort Churchill |
| Spring | **4** Wild Rose Trail |
| | **5** Bear Canyon Suspension Bridge |
| | **7** Stewart Falls |
| | **9** Fifth Water Hot Springs |
| | **19** Goblin Valley |
| | **20** Hickman Natural Bridge |
| | **24** Panorama Point Trail |
| | **31** Cascade Falls |
| | **32** Hidden Haven Falls |
| | **33** Timber Creek Overlook |
| | **34** The Watchman |
| | **35** Zion Canyon Overlook |
| | **40** Calico Tanks |
| | **48** Monkey Rock |
| | **50** Mary Jane Falls |

**Summer**

- (1) Limber Pine Nature Trail
- (6) Donut Falls
- (10) Mirror Lake
- (25) Queens Garden
- (26) Bristlecone Pine Loop
- (44) Smith Lake
- (46) Spooner Lake
- (48) Monkey Rock

**Fall**

- (2) Icebox Canyon
- (3) Buffalo Point
- (8) Maple Canyon Arch
- (9) Fifth Water Hot Springs
- (11) Dinosaur Tracks at Red Fleet State Park
- (16) Hovenweep Ruins
- (18) Sipapu Natural Bridge
- (19) Goblin Valley
- (21) Sunset Point
- (23) Lower Calf Creek Falls
- (27) Red Hollow
- (33) Timber Creek Overlook
- (41) Cathedral Gorge
- (42) Alpine Lakes
- (45) Griffith Canyon Petroglyphs
- (46) Spooner Lake
- (47) Fort Churchill

# PREPARING FOR YOUR ADVENTURE

A great trail is a story—it has a beginning, a true climax or crux, and then an end, whether back the way you came or wrapping up in a loop. After a hike, read the maps with your children and encourage them to feel the story of the trail. How did you like the beginning? What was the climax? How did it end? What characters were on the trail, the trees or animals that stood out to them? Another fun post-hike activity is taking your nature journal and writing a fictional account of what happened on the trail, making the landscape come alive in a whole new way. By helping children interpret the experience, you extend the magic that happened on the trail and create the thirst for more!

# INDIVIDUAL ADVENTURE PROFILES

This guide is a starter pack to a life full of adventure with your young ones, taking you to the far corners of both Utah and Nevada. Imagine—one day, your adventurers will be calling you up and asking if you want to hike to the top of Kings Peak, the tallest mountain in Utah. Our parents took us hiking before we could walk, and now it's something we still love to do together. Hailey's mom even came along on her son's first backpacking trip, and we hope to do the same with our own grandkids someday.

Each of the fifty adventure profiles includes a basic trail map and information on the species of plants and wildlife, points of historical interest, and geological features that you may see on the trail. By allowing children to navigate using the maps and route elevation guides, read the hike and species descriptions, and look for each featured item like a scavenger hunt, you're fostering the building blocks of adventure. Marking journeys on the map with these points of interest gives relevance and context to kids' surroundings, so encourage them to note areas that stood out to them as well. You'll burst with pride when kids start to teach you what a lollipop loop is versus an out and back, are able to gauge whether they feel like just kicking it on a hike with 200 feet of elevation gain or tackling 1000 feet, and make decisions about their own adventure trail. Each is written for both you and the kids, so encourage them to read to themselves or out loud to you.

## Elevation profile, length, type of trail, and time

The elevation profile graph is a line that sketches the general arch of the up-and-down during the hike. You'll notice a few are almost completely flat, and some are nearly a triangle. The elevation listed is how many feet you'll gain from start to finish; so even if it rolls up and then down again, if it says 300 feet that will be the total number of feet you'll gain from the trailhead to the summit.

Only one adventure (Calf Creek Falls) is more than 5 miles, making them accessible for our younger or newer adventurers. The length of these hikes should give you plenty of time to enjoy the outing before anyone gets too tired. Embracing shorter trails—a couple are less than 1 mile—translates into more time to savor the adventure.

Talking with kids about the type of trail you're planning to hike will help young adventurers know what's coming and what to expect. Along with the length of the trail, we note whether the adventure is an out and back, a loop, or a lollipop loop and whether a clockwise or counter-clockwise route is recommended.

 An out and back has a clear final destination and turnaround point, and you'll cross back over what you've already discovered.

 A loop provides brand new territory the whole way around.

 A lollipop is a straight line with a mini-loop at the end, like reaching a lake and then circling it, and heading back.

The estimated hike time includes time for exploration. Always give yourselves the delight of a relaxing hike with plenty of time to stop and play with a pile of fun-looking rocks, have leaf-boat races on a stream, or sketch a bird.

## Level of difficulty

This rating system was designed to facilitate having a good time. It's important to note that these are kid-centric ratings; what's labeled as a "challenging" trail in this guide may not appear to be so challenging for a seasoned adult hiker. It can be fun to create your own rating for a trail when you're finished. "Did that feel like a level 1, 2, or 3 to you? Why?" Talking about it can help you understand kids' adventure limits or help them seek new challenges. None of the trails in this book are paved—at least not all the way—but some are level and smooth. Due to the geological history of Utah and Nevada, most have some combination of rocks and roots.

We note if there are exposed ledges or viewpoints where you'll want to hold smaller hands.

The rockier terrain will cry for some sturdy shoes, and you'll want to find out how wet, muddy, or snowy it may be to inform your decision of which pair will be best for your kids. It can help if you check reviews on AllTrails.com to get recent conditions and families' opinions of the difficulty. While scouting these trails with our families, we saw many walking toddlers, strollers of every tire type imaginable, and baby backpacks on even the most challenging trails. We also spotted a couple of sport strollers on moderately rocky trails with exposed roots. Use the information here to make informed decisions, bold adventurers.

The adventures are rated as follows:

- **EASY** These trails are typically short (1 mile or so), have low elevation gain, have even non-rocky terrain, and don't have too many exposed/handholding ledges.

- **MODERATE** These adventures have a bit more elevation gain (300 feet or so) and are likely to have a few handholding spots for the youngest hikers. The terrain itself may also be a bit rockier or rootier.

- **CHALLENGING** These adventures will give your little adventurers the biggest sense of accomplishment. These have the most elevation gain (300 to 1100 feet), and some have sections where you'll probably want kids to stay close as they take in an exposed view. If they're steeper, however, they'll also be shorter—more than doable with the right attitude and by taking advantage of power-up stops and the adrenaline-inducing rush of finding special scavenger hunt items.

## Season

This section lists the season when the adventure is possible; in many cases, the trails can be hiked year-round. We also note the seasons when features of special interest can be seen, such as wildflowers or rushing waterfalls.

The long stretch of Nevada's Highway 50, dubbed the "Loneliest Road of America," offers spectacular views of the Basin and Range topography and opportunities to see wildlife too

In winter and early spring, check with the local agency listed for each hike to make sure the trail and access road is actually open. In general, the higher up you go, the more likely you could be closed out by snow on either side of summer. Some adventures lend themselves to snow exploration without any gear, whereas others are a great time to try snowshoes or snow tracks on your shoes if you're so inclined.

Phenology is the study of how plants change across the seasons, and hikers are often the first to notice when leaves change colors or when a certain flower starts to bloom. Try taking the same hike in several seasons to teach your little adventurers about differences in the seasons, particularly for flora and fauna. The more often you go, the more likely you are to find something you may have missed the last time.

## Get there

When Wendy was seven, her dad took the family out for their first off-roading experience in a small white Toyota pickup in the California desert. Their truck was promptly lodged between two rocks and got towed out six hours later. Although that experience built some character and an adventurous spirit in Wendy, these kinds of roads are not included in this guide. These adventures have all been road-tested at least once and specifically target trailheads with fairly easy access, meaning minimal dirt, gravel, or pothole-strewn roads. We'll leave those to our seasoned adventurers.

Utah and Nevada are big, adventurers. Almost 200,000 square miles! We hope that you and your children flip through and dream of one day taking a road trip along the "Loneliest Road in America", Highway 50 in Nevada, or heading to the southernmost stretches of Utah and finding ancient ruins at Bears Ears National Monument. Car rides are a necessity to reach this amazing buffet of hikes available to you, and we hope you embrace the special family time that road trips can offer your crew. It's worth the drive to make it to one of the furthest sections of eastern Utah to explore the abandoned city of Hovenweep or to stop by historic charcoal ovens that helped power Nevada's robust mining industry. The memories made on your road trips will last a lifetime—Wendy and Hailey fondly remember the long drives their families took them on at an early age to reach hikes.

You have your screen of choice, of course, but consider a few fun ways to make the hours fly by fast, such as riddles, the A–Z game (you claim every time you see something that starts with the next letter of the alphabet), audiobooks, call-and-response type camp songs (bit.ly/TimberSongs), nature journaling, and just good old-fashioned conversation. Always be ready to roll down the windows for fresh air, and encourage your little riders to look at the horizon if they start to get carsick.

Most of these hikes are verified awesome spots in the midst of even more to explore! Consider making a camping trip out of it. We also encourage you to stop by visitor centers, many of which have Junior Ranger

This adventurer has collected a lot of Junior Ranger badges!

programs. Be sure to get your passport stamp at the national parks and ask if they have a Junior Ranger program; the parks often have an activity book that, once completed, nets a sweet badge for your adventure bag.

Each adventure comes with a case-sensitive Google Maps link you can drop directly into your browser that will provide directions to the trailhead on your smartphone. Just be sure to do it before you head out, while you are still certain to have coverage. You also can download offline maps at Google Maps and the AllTrails app for free, which will allow you to follow your GPS dot and ensure you're staying on the trail or road you want to be on. Basic directions to each trailhead are also listed. You can get free highway maps mailed to you or printed, which can be helpful and educational for your copilot in the car (check the tourism website for each state: VisitUtah.com and NVCulture.org). You and your kids can also geek out on Google Earth or turn Google Maps' satellite view on to walk your road (and sometimes even trail) step by step.

There's something magical about maps. Each physical map in this guide was carefully designed with kids in mind to be touched, traced, and held out in front of them to understand the land around them. Encourage your kids to understand the difference between roads, highways, and interstate freeways. Even-numbered roads, for instance, run east and west, and odd-numbered ones run north and south. We've simplified the maps so kids can focus on the points of interest, directions, and turns and begin building vital map-reading skills. Hopefully they start to build a sixth sense of understanding how to navigate using maps while they adventure with you. Just by asking questions, you can encourage curiosity and leadership in your young adventurers: How long will this adventure take, do you think?

Where does that river start, and how is it related to the ocean? How many turns will we need to make? What's our next highway? Any cities nearby? Any fun names you can see?

## Restrooms

We can't have a hiking book for kids without chatting about bathrooms. Many of the trails have pit toilets or developed toilets right at the parking lot. If not, plan on a restroom stop in the nearest town or gas station on your way in and way out. Discuss appropriate trail bathroom etiquette with your kids as well, such as heading safely off the trail, away from water, and properly covering it should the need arise. Bring what you need to be comfortable in your adventure bag, such as a Ziploc bag with toilet paper. Don't leave any toilet paper behind to spoil someone else's experience; make sure to pack it back out.

## Parking and fees

Your main goal, lead adventurers, is to get out on the trail. If thinking about how to park and pay gets your boot laces knotted up, rest assured. All the trailheads listed here have a parking lot or pull-out and some sort of trail sign indicating where you are and whether you need a parking pass or permit. For some, you'll need to plan ahead and get a day pass or annual pass before you get to the trailhead. Others have self-service pay stations at the trailhead—either those accepting credit cards or an iron ranger with a slot in it for a fee envelope with cash or check—and you'll affix the pass to your car. Many parking lots are free, while others are free for in-state residents but have a fee for out-of-state visitors. There are several fee-free days including National Public Lands Day in September and many holidays. If you're wondering whether these day or annual passes are worth it, they most certainly are. We were able to witness firsthand during the winter how safe the staff and rangers keep trails at the ready for us and our families, and these fees pay for that maintenance.

## Treat yourself

To reward yourselves, the guide lists nearby cafes and restaurants for good, quick bites, in part so you can plan whether you need to pack substantial snacks or just a few with you on the trail. These are road-tested yummy bakeries, ice cream shops, burger joints, and family-friendly breweries with notable items or spaces that your kids will enjoy.

## Managing agencies

The name of the agency that manages each of the hiking trails is given, along with the telephone number and Facebook handle (which is also usually its Twitter and Instagram handle). Before heading out, it's a good idea to check on current conditions, including weather, roads, wildlife sightings, and any hazards that haven't been cleared or fixed. The folks on the other end are often rangers and are generally thrilled to share information about their trails. They can also connect you to botanists, geologists, historians, and more. We received such fast and enthusiastic responses from many of the rangers behind the Facebook pages of these parks. Involve your kids, and encourage them to say hello and ask about conditions or any unanswered questions they had on the trail.

## Scavenger hunts

The scavenger hunt in each adventure invites you to look for specific fungi, plants, animals, minerals, and historical items of interest. You'll find descriptions and photos of trees, leaves, flowers, cones, wildlife or animal tracks, rocks and geological features, historically significant landmarks or artifacts, natural features such as lakes and rivers and waterfalls, or culturally significant spots that appear on each trail. Each entry has a question to ponder or an activity to try; when applicable, you can dig into the scientific genus and species and learn why the plant or animal is called what it is. Encourage kids to preview what they might see on the trail; if they think they've found it, take out the map to match. Take it up a notch and encourage them to make their own scavenger hunt—write down five things they think they might see on the trail today, from very basic (at least five trees) to the very specific (five juniper berries on the ground).

# IDENTIFYING WHAT YOU FIND

Utah and Nevada are full of living things! Identifying species of plants, fungi, birds, mammals, invertebrates, reptiles, and amphibians in the wild involves using clues such as habitat, sounds, color, size, leaves, bark, and flowers. Work with kids to ask questions that will move them from general identification (Is it a conifer or a deciduous tree?) to the specifics (What shape are the leaves? What does the bark look like?). The species of trees, shrubs, mushrooms, wildflowers, and animals listed in the scavenger hunts were chosen because you should be able to find them with ease and there's something interesting about them that might appeal to children. You may not find every species on the trail every time, however. It's best to adopt the attitude of considering it a win when you do find one and to present those you can't find as something to look forward to next time.

Tristan Gooley, British author of *The Natural Navigator*, encourages kids to look for keys as they walk on trails. "Keys are small families of clues and signs. If we focus on them repeatedly, it can give us a sixth sense." Start noticing which way the sun is when you start and when you end, as well as where the natural features (hills, mountains) are around you, and use the compass on your smartphone to start understanding direction and building this natural sixth sense that Gooley speaks of.

When you find a particularly interesting species on the trail that's not mentioned in the scavenger hunt, have kids either sketch or take a photo of it. Remind them to look it up later, either in a printed field guide to the region or on a specialty website such as WildflowerSearch.com. You can even use Google Image Search to drop in your photo and compare it to similar images. You can look it up on iNaturalist.org or download the

Encourage kids to pick up and investigate the items they find and try to identify them

*Look at the things you encounter from different scales and different angles and different parts. Say a tree—you have a really large organism and you might need to stand really far away to see a picture of it. But look closer— and find the fruit on the ground, look at the bark, look at the leaves. Think of all the different characteristics that can help you learn what it is, why it lives where it is. Start recognizing all of the pieces of an organism and thinking how to capture those photographically if you want to share that record with the world. Try to find the part of the thing that is most unique-looking and try to fill the frame with that.*

—Carrie Seltzer, iNaturalist

Seek by iNaturalist or LeafSnap apps to treasure hunt species on the trail. Adding basic descriptions and the name of the region will help in trying to find your treasure in online field guides.

If you're ready to level up everyone's identification skills, join the Native Plant Trust (NativePlantTrust .org), the Nevada Native Plant Society (NVNPS.org), and the Utah Native Plant Society (UNPS.org). All have great Facebook groups, newsletters, and/or online forums where you can share when species start to bloom or a photo of a species you can't identify. Joining your local chapter also means getting invited to their fun group hikes on topics such as wildflowers or fungi and everything in between. You'll be exposing your kids to the power of a community resource where everyone is passionate about nature and science and wants to help each other out. The USA National Phenology Network (USANPN.org) allows kids to contribute to actual science by entering their observation of seasonal changes into a nationwide database, and it has a cool Junior Phenologist Program and kid-friendly resources to boot.

Kids are natural-born climbers; let them stop and climb on the bounty of rocks you'll come across

Portions of three geological provinces—the Basin and Range, the Colorado Plateau, and the Rocky Mountains—lie within Utah and Nevada's boundaries. No wonder these states boast such scenery! The massive metamorphic rocks of the Uinta Mountains of the Rocky Mountain province contrast markedly with the red, flat-layered rocks of the mesas of the Colorado Plateau and the gray, folded, faulted, complex mountain-blocks of the Basin and Range. Processes of erosion dominate the Colorado Plateau today, while sedimentation dominates the Basin and Range. This region is a very cool place to explore rocks and geology, and you'll notice some amazing sights in the adventures in this guide.

While encountering these cool colors, folds, and structures, encourage children to think about the general rock cycle—a rock's evolution from igneous (melted rock) to metamorphic to sedimentary—and how it builds up in deposits over time. Use the scavenger hunts to start to build a familiarity with Utah's red rocks so your kids can start to find them and notice the subtle differences. Ask questions: What does the texture of the rock look like? What color is it? Does it feel heavy or light? Is it hard or soft? Does it break easily?

You can also join a regional geological society like the Utah Geological Survey (Geology.Utah.gov) and the Geological Society of Nevada (GSNV.org) for newsletters, group hikes, and community opportunities.

*Nevada is the fastest growing state, tectonically speaking. We add a couple of acres a year as the plates pull apart and stretch, making all the mountain ranges and the flat basin. Nevada has the most mountain ranges of any state! When I was growing up, I started reading* National Geographic *about plate tectonics and collected rocks, and then I realized there is a field called geology and I can do something with a passionate hobby. I encourage parents to help kids "follow their bliss." If your kids like rocks, bring along a hand lens or small rock hammer to investigate and help them develop a deeper interest in rocks. Ask questions like "What does this look like close up? When you break it, why do the fresh surfaces look different from the weathered surfaces?"*

—James Faulds, PhD, Nevada State Geologist

# HISTORICAL ITEMS

This 1857 map of Utah and New Mexico Territories was drafted before Utah became a state

People have been living in Utah and Nevada for thousands of years, and there are many signs of ancient civilizations and relics from the Old West to be found. Each state and even regions within a state often have their own historical society with resources and an email and phone number to ask questions. Join your local historical society to start to identify items of historical interest on Utah and Nevada's trails: Utah State Historical Society (History.Utah.gov) and Nevada Historical Society (NVHistorical Society.org). Parents can foster inquiry with each hike.

Kids love to explore historical places, like the Ward Charcoal Ovens in Nevada

Folks came into this region from all over the world as long as 13,000 years ago—it's called "The Crossroads of the West" for good reason! It's easy to see the trail as something that's always been present, but so much history has taken place here, thinking of the generations of the people who have passed through. Let kids know that other people have moved across this landscape for many years, and it was the homelands of Indigenous peoples. The place is not yours—it's everybody's. It's a special place that other people have considered to be home. I encourage families to identify land use changes as they walk the trail to understand its history: Have trees been cut down? Do you see any evidence of any kind of mining? Do you see any evidence of people once living here? What do you see in how the land has been changed by humans?

—Jedediah Rogers, Utah State Historian

# POWER-UP STOPS

Liz Thomas has hiked more than 15,000 miles and is the former speed record holder for the Appalachian Trail. Her biggest tip for young adventurers to build stamina? "Understand your body. Kids are just figuring out how to read their bodies. You can think of your body as having gauges and you're the pilot at the front of the plane. Your goal is to keep your gauges (hydration, exposure, food) in the happy zone." She even sets reminders on her watch to drink and eat as she walks from sunrise to sunset. As lead adventurers, you'll be keeping a close eye on these gauges but also helping kids recognize them, anticipate them, and power through them.

For each adventure, we note key places that serve as mini-milestones or power-up stops. Be sure to pack snacks for your kids to eat at these stops to keep blood sugar, energy levels, and mood high, as this amount of physical activity may be challenging for little ones. Don't underestimate the power of choosing a special snack to serve as a particular motivator on tough ascents or rainy days.

Often, these power-up stops come before switchbacks up a hill or are at points of interest, like fun bridges or overlooking a viewpoint. Stopping for a moment can fuel you up, give you a chance to listen to the wind and the animals around you, watch what's going on, and prepare for the larger goal of finishing the adventure itself. Power-up stops

Bridges make great stops to just relax and explore

can also be great for a nursing mom or a bottle-feeding caregiver or for tending to other little ones' needs, as well as for question-based games like "I Spy." As the lead adventurer, use these stops for inspiration, play, questions, games, and riddles and encourage your kids to do the same.

# ADVENTURE BAG, SUPPLIES, AND SAFETY

Start your kids on a lifelong habit of packing an adventure bag, whether it's the smallest satchel or the largest consumer-grade backpack they can actually hold. The art of having everything you need with you without being too burdened is key to having a good time on the trail. All the adventures are short enough that even if you did pack too much, its weight won't jeopardize your enjoyment levels too heavily. Review the trail location, its length, and proximity to town and decide what your team needs to feel comfortable and safe.

REI advocates ten essentials to hiking, which can be a great way of introducing self-sufficiency to your kids. Involve kids in packing these items and understanding what they're for.

**NAVIGATION** Keep your smartphone charged for access to offline maps and the compass feature. In addition to the maps in this book, consider a compass and full trail map of the area (GreenTrailsMaps.com).

**HYDRATION** Bring plenty of water for everyone.

**NUTRITION** Consider the length of the trail and the amount and type of snacks you'll need to keep going.

**FIRE** Pack a lighter or matchbook for emergencies.

**FIRST AID KIT** This can range from a mini first aid kit with essentials such as bandages and aspirin to much heftier options with space blankets. Consider what you want your car stocked with and what you want on the trail with you.

Some trails are fully exposed to the hot desert sun, so take appropriate precautions

- **TOOLS** A small knife or multi-tool goes a long way on the trail.

- **ILLUMINATION** Did you explore just a wee bit too long and dusk is approaching? A simple headlamp, flashlight, or even your phone's flashlight can help lead the way.

- **SUN AND INSECT PROTECTION** If it's an exposed trail, bring sunglasses and sunscreen or hats. In the summer, many trails may have biting insects, so be prepared with your favorite method of repelling them.

- **SHELTER** You may want a space blanket or small tarp in your adventure bag in case of emergency.

- **INSULATION** Check the weather together and decide the type of protection and warmth you want to bring. A second layer is always a good idea; breezes can chill even the warmest of days.

Even if you pack everything, things can and will go wrong sometimes. Lenore Skenazy, president of Let Grow—a nonprofit promoting independence as a critical part of childhood—and founder of the Free-Range Kids movement, has this reply about handling the inevitable fear of shepherding your family on adventures:

*I'm often asked, "What if something goes wrong?" I love to ask back, "Can anyone remember something that went wrong when you were a kid, playing with other kids?" People often look back so fondly on that time when things went wrong. There's even a word for the way we treasure imperfect things and moments: kintsugi, from the Japanese practice of filling a crack in a vase— an imperfection—with gold, because the imperfection is what makes it beautiful. The outdoors is never without some surprises and even minor risks, but neither is the indoors. My guess is you all can remember when something went wrong and it is a treasured (if only in retrospect!) memory. Imperfection is inevitable and valuable. Embrace it!*

Fun items to have on hand might include a nature journal and pen/pencil, hand lens, binoculars, a camera, a super-special treat for when you reach the top of something, and even a favorite figurine or toy that your littles are currently enamored with so they interact with that tree stump up ahead. Wet wipes, toilet paper, and Ziploc bags are also recommended. First-timer? Join a hiking group like Hike it Baby or Sierra Club to hike with your peers and learn the ropes of packing.

While it may be handy for you to navigate to each trailhead using your smartphone, remember that many of these wilderness areas have spotty cell service. As a general safety practice for hiking with kids, always tell a third party where you are going and when you expect to be back, and remember to tell anyone who may need to get a hold of you while you're away that you're not certain of cell coverage in the area.

On the trail itself, every lead adventurer will have his or her own comfort level with safety, and you'll determine when your children will need handholding or reminders to stay close as you get near tricky terrain, exposed edges, or water. It's a given in the diversity of climates in Utah and Nevada that you can come across adverse weather conditions arriving seemingly out of nowhere. Teaching awareness and common sense and fostering an attitude of "there's no bad weather, only the wrong clothing" in these situations will go a long way toward creating an adventurous and resilient child. You can model this "love the unlovable" attitude by remaining upbeat and playful as lead adventurer, and you'll be amazed at how quickly their attention will turn back to the trail and its wonders.

Poison oak is a common hazard lurking around in wooded areas of Utah and Nevada. Once you learn to identify it, you'll soon be able to spot it right

Poison oak (*Toxicodendron diversilobum*)

away on the trail. Touching this plant will cause a blistering rash in most people. Each branch of this woody vine or shrub has three shiny lobed leaflets. The leaves are usually bronze when first unfolding, bright green in the spring, yellow-green to reddish in the summer, and bright red or pink in late summer and fall.

Western rattlesnakes (*Crotalus viridis*), black bears (*Ursus americanus*), and mountain lions/cougars (*Puma concolor*) are other hazards that come with the call of adventure in Utah and Nevada. Rattlesnakes likely will be hanging out by their den (rocks) and will not want to bother you, so give a wide berth as you walk around them and don't poke your hands into rock crevices. If you see a bear, try not to freak out—simply hold your ground and slowly back up, raising your arms to appear larger—as they are not typically aggressive. Do be sure to pick up any of your smaller hikers with you, like toddlers.

If you cross paths with a cougar, you'll want to make yourself large, shout, and scare the cat away. Do *not* run, because running stimulates a cougar's instinct to chase. Blacklegged ticks are another animal to watch out for in wooded areas. Make a habit of doing a tick check on everyone after leaving a trail with a fair amount of vegetation. If you do find a tick, use tweezers to grasp the tick by the head (not the body) as close to the skin as possible and lift up. In areas where you may encounter these animals, trailheads usually have reminders of their presence and the precautions to take. By helping kids be aware on the trail, looking for signs of wildlife, and knowing what to do when they come across them, you can create a lifelong safety skill set for adventuring.

Be sure to read all the trailhead signs, as in the fall and winter there can be hunting permitted near the land you explore. At these places, you'll want to wear bright orange on your head and body. We call out specific trails that this applies to, but it's always good to research this on other trails you might encounter.

Summer warmth brings thunderstorms. Particularly in the mountains in Utah and Nevada, you might see one form almost every afternoon in July and August. Be sure to check the forecast, and if there's any rain or thunder forecasted, stay home. If you do happen to get a fast storm come upon you, avoid water, avoid high ground or exposed mountaintops, and avoid all metal objects including fences. Crouch down, put your feet together, and avoid proximity to other people. Unsafe places include underneath canopies, small picnic or rain shelters, or near trees. Where possible, find shelter in a substantial building or in a fully enclosed metal vehicle such as a car, truck, or van with the windows completely shut.

It's important to avoid hiking near narrow canyons if rain is forecast. Flash floods can happen even from storms far away, so be sure to check in with the visitor center to see if any are forecast before heading out. Many people describe the sound of an oncoming flash flood as like a train, a rumble, thunder, or loud wind. If you hear something like this, seek higher ground *immediately*. These potentially deadly floods move fast.

When hiking at higher elevations, take it slow and drink more water than normal. Be alert for the symptoms of altitude mountain sickness— headaches, rapid breath, vomiting, and fatigue—which can happen over 8000 feet. If anyone in your party feels this, have them put their head down, drink water, and eat food and seek medical attention if the symptoms persist.

# NATURE JOURNALING

Wendy received her first nature journal in Sydney, Australia, on her first night as a National Geographic Fellow with a group of students and teachers from around the world. It was leather-bound and bursting with empty pages, just begging to be doodled and written in.

Catherine Hughes, retired head of the *National Geographic Kids* magazine education team, gently guides us with a few key maxims for nature journaling:

- **Make quick, messy field notes.** You can add details later when you have free time, like the drive home. You don't have to be a great artist to sketch something you see.

- **Sketch the map of the adventure that day.**

- **Personalize it.** Did someone say something funny? What was the most unique thing that happened on the adventure?

- **Use it like a scrapbook.** Add trail brochures and tickets to your journal to remember your adventure.

Consider picking out a small blank journal for kids to bring along in their adventure bags. At power-up stops, when you stop for lunch at the destination, on the ride home, or later that night, encourage your little adventurers to create drawings of things they saw, document their observations of trees or animals, and press leaves or flowers.

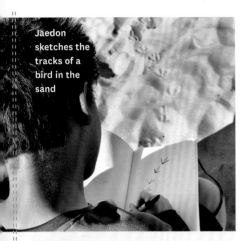

Jaedon sketches the tracks of a bird in the sand

*One of my favorite techniques is to take one flower, branch, or leaf and draw it from several different angles. Each time you rotate, you'll notice new details you didn't see before. Or you can create interesting compositions by drawing and layering multiple stages of a plant like buds, fallen petals, and full blooms. Similarly, when I draw animals, I often blend their natural patterns into the textures that surround them. Feathers, wings, petals, and leaves play together to create dizzying but satisfying patterns. It's like a game of hide-and-seek to discover where one plant or animal ends and another begins.*

—Maggie Enterrios, author of *Nature Observer*

# DIGITAL CONNECTIONS

The social media accounts of many of the agencies that manage public lands are quite active, and they can be a great way for kids to use technology to enhance their experience in nature. They can ask pre- or post-adventure questions about conditions or flora and fauna, and the forums can be wonderful vehicles for sharing images you snapped—for both you and your little adventurer. Search the location on Instagram for recent photos, and be sure to geotag yours to contribute to other hikers' searches as well.

Enhance the journey and encourage kids to define what really stood out to them about the experience with a co-authored trip report on one of these sites.

**AllTrails.com** This a crowd-sourced database of hikes built by a community of 4 million registered members that includes reviews and user-uploaded photos. Kids can add their starred reviews, photos, and comments after they hike and help out the community, and they can search for kid-friendly hikes or by feature and save them to a list.

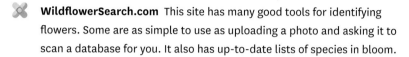 **WildflowerSearch.com**  This site has many good tools for identifying flowers. Some are as simple to use as uploading a photo and asking it to scan a database for you. It also has up-to-date lists of species in bloom.

 **iNaturalist.org and Seek by iNaturalist**  This web- and app-based online community allows you to share your species observations with other naturalists around the world. It's also a great place to post a question if you can't identify something you found.

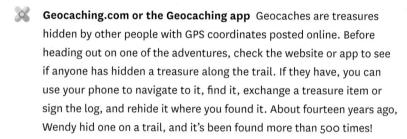 **Geocaching.com or the Geocaching app**  Geocaches are treasures hidden by other people with GPS coordinates posted online. Before heading out on one of the adventures, check the website or app to see if anyone has hidden a treasure along the trail. If they have, you can use your phone to navigate to it, find it, exchange a treasure item or sign the log, and rehide it where you found it. About fourteen years ago, Wendy hid one on a trail, and it's been found more than 500 times!

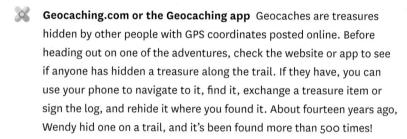 **HikeitBaby.com**  This online community promotes group hikes with other families of small children. Everyone is there for the same thing— to get babies outside. You can find your local community on the website's Communities tab, which will have the Facebook group for a specific city, like Salt Lake City and Las Vegas, and the city's ambassadors.

# SMARTPHONES

You may have picked up this book to find ways of distracting kids from their phones. You already know where you stand on the issue of screen time, but if letting kids use their phone on the trail to take a photo of an interesting flower, navigate with a digital compass app, use the audio app to capture a birdsong, or share their photos of the hike on the park's Instagram on the drive home sounds like a conscientious way to bridge technology and outdoor time, go for it. Of course, not using a phone at all can be equally fun and appropriate.

Sara McCarty, founder of Run Wild My Child, has this advice for families: "Continue to encourage your kids to try new things, like hiking with you. You're never going to know what they're going to like or try. The reason kids want to be on screens is because of connection and socialization—get them outside with a friend and they'll be way more likely to stay outside." You can connect with other families by using the Run Wild My Child website to find new outdoor activities to try and share your adventures with the #runwildmychild Instagram community.

# CAMPING AND BACKPACKING

Extending the adventure by camping and backpacking can be an amazing next step to day hiking with your family. Backpacking with a baby is not for the faint of heart, but it's such a rewarding experience if you're willing to put the work in. If you've ever gone backpacking before, you know that how much weight you're carrying can greatly impact how much you enjoy the trip. Too much heavy gear can really wear you down and make it a grueling experience. So when Hailey brought her baby along, she made sure to only bring necessities and be as minimal as possible. Minimal has a whole different meaning, though, when going in the backcountry with kids.

Diapers are an important thing for every baby. Before Hailey's family went on the trip, they took note of how many diapers they were using a day so they knew how many to pack, with a few spares. Carrying them out was a little tough, but a couple things that helped were leaving a little bit of space in their packs knowing used diapers would take up more space and letting the diapers dry out at camp to allow some of the moisture to evaporate. If you are in an area where you don't need to carry out all of your waste, you can bury the poop (not the diaper) in a 6-inch-deep hole.

Another big question is finding the right setup to carry your baby. While Hailey's first child was little, they preferred carrying him in a framed

Many campsites are close to the trailhead with beautiful surroundings, like this one at Lower Calf Creek in Utah

child carrier while her partner carried most of their gear. The Osprey Poco Plus has the most storage of any child carrier on the market currently, and they were able to fit a decent amount of gear in there. Another option is to carry your regular backpack while wearing your child in a soft carrier on the front. This way you have a lot more storage space.

Backpacking isn't for everyone, and if you're interested in bringing a little more gear, car camping is a fun option that we love! One thing that has made our camping and backpacking experiences easier with a kid is the Morrison Outdoors sleeping bag. It's a safe sleep option for kids from 6 months to 4 years old. It's basically a sleep sack with sleeves made out of sleeping bag materials. They have bags rated for 20°F and 40°F. Another piece of clothing that we love for all our trips is a fleece bunting. It's warm, dirt brushes off easily, and it won't hold onto moisture like cotton does.

# SHOWING RESPECT FOR NATURE

Utah and Nevada are home to 6 million people, and enjoying and protecting the land in this region will be key to conserving its beauty for generations to come. You're doing the most important thing you can to keep these places beautiful: taking your kids outside. We are inspiring stewards—the more we are out there understanding and delighting in the natural world with our families, the more we and our little adventurers will want to take care of it in the future. This region in particular boasts some of the most fragile artifacts in the world, including petroglyphs, pictographs, and dinosaur tracks from long ago. Teaching your kids to respect these amazing clues from the past is paramount to them remaining for their kids to see and enjoy one day.

You can't help but feel a part of something larger when you get yourself on top of a peak or squeeze through the Red Hollow slot canyon with your kids. Simply by noticing and beginning to identify features, flora, and fauna in nature, you're creating a sense of respect and appreciation. Model and embrace the "leave no trace" ethos (see LNT.org for more great ideas) on each and every trail. Be diligent with snack wrappers and the flotsam and jetsam of your adventure bag. Some of the beautiful areas in this guide are also the most remote and precious, so please stay on the trail. Avoid trampling vegetation and disturbing wildlife to ensure that everyone and everything can share these amazing places.

Conservation is also easier than ever before. When she was a teacher in Los Angeles, Wendy's classroom adopted a Mojave Desert tortoise and a California Channel Island fox and committed to educating their school about them. They raised money to support their survival and used real-world GPS data to track them and make deductions about their behavior and living with humans. Invite your kids to see if they can help with citizen science by reporting observations back to ranger stations, cleaning up trash, and volunteering to maintain trails.

As young naturalists, the scavenger hunts will be asking kids to notice, to touch, and to play with nature around them in a safe and gentle way.

For the most part, try not to take a leaf or flower off of a growing plant, but rather collect and play with items that are already on the ground. Manipulate them, stack them, create art with them, trace them in journals—but then leave them to be used by the other creatures on the trail, from the fungi decomposing a leaf to another kid walking down the trail tomorrow. Many of these wilderness areas and public lands were created with leaders in Utah and Nevada, and you're creating the next generation of conservationists simply by getting kids out in nature.

A good winter setup is crucial to enjoying the cold weather

# ADVENTURES IN
## UTAH

*Adventurers,* let's begin in the Beehive State on the historic homelands of the Shoshone, Goshute, Ute, Ancestral Puebloans, and Fremont. We'll start in the Salt Lake City area and then work our way through the Rocky Mountains and end up on the 11,000-foot-high Colorado Plateau. We'll hike to a huge pine tree, explore a cool canyon, look for bison, and cross a historical suspension bridge. There are trips to waterfalls and hot springs and a chance to follow ancient dinosaur tracks. Utah's Grand Staircase of geological layers offers lots of cool features for us to explore. We'll start at Arches National Park, where we'll climb a slickrock whale, and then take in the view at Canyonlands National Park. We'll visit an ancient village in a canyon at Hovenweep National Monument. We'll cross under natural bridges, find rocky goblins, play in Devils Garden, take in the colorful spires of Kodachrome Basin, head up a slot canyon, climb through caves, bound across pink coral sand dunes, find rocky toadstools, and even explore an old lava flow. There's so much to see in Utah—let's go!

# 1

# LOOK FOR THE LIMBER PINE

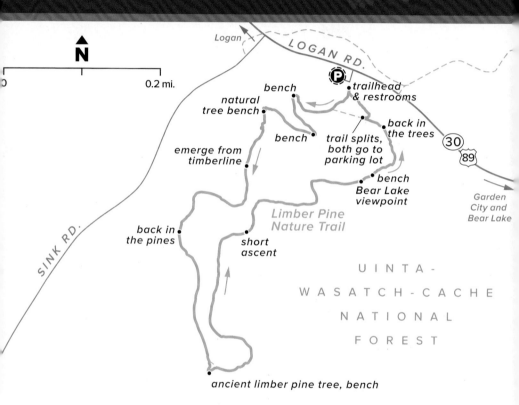

Logan

**LOGAN RD.**

bench

P trailhead & restrooms

**N**

0                    0.2 mi.

natural tree bench

bench

back in the trees

30

89

emerge from timberline

trail splits, both go to parking lot

bench
Bear Lake viewpoint

*Limber Pine Nature Trail*

Garden City and Bear Lake

SINK RD.

back in the pines

short ascent

UINTA-

WASATCH-CACHE

NATIONAL

FOREST

ancient limber pine tree, bench

## YOUR ADVENTURE

Adventurers, today you're on the historical homelands of the Eastern Shoshone-Bannock in the 2.2 million–acre Uinta-Wasatch-Cache National Forest. (The word *uinta* means "pine tree," *wasatch* means "low place in high mountains," and *cache* is a French word for caves used by trappers to hide their furs.) Begin heading right on the Limber Pine Nature Trail to

This limber pine is actually a network of five trees all grown together →

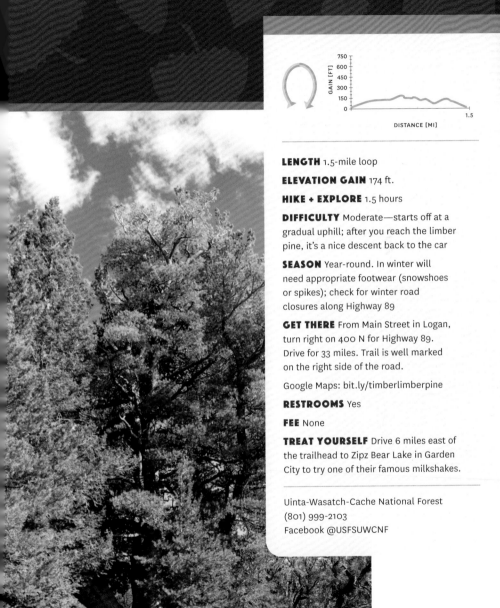

GAIN [FT]

750
600
450
300
150
0

DISTANCE [MI]    1.5

**LENGTH** 1.5-mile loop

**ELEVATION GAIN** 174 ft.

**HIKE + EXPLORE** 1.5 hours

**DIFFICULTY** Moderate—starts off at a gradual uphill; after you reach the limber pine, it's a nice descent back to the car

**SEASON** Year-round. In winter will need appropriate footwear (snowshoes or spikes); check for winter road closures along Highway 89

**GET THERE** From Main Street in Logan, turn right on 400 N for Highway 89. Drive for 33 miles. Trail is well marked on the right side of the road.

Google Maps: bit.ly/timberlimberpine

**RESTROOMS** Yes

**FEE** None

**TREAT YOURSELF** Drive 6 miles east of the trailhead to Zipz Bear Lake in Garden City to try one of their famous milkshakes.

Uinta-Wasatch-Cache National Forest
(801) 999-2103
Facebook @USFSUWCNF

take a counterclockwise loop at a gradual incline as you hike among pine trees and aspens. You'll pass by a couple of benches that are great spots to enjoy the scenery of Logan Canyon or power up if you need to. Before long, you'll be out of the cover of the pines under the wide-open sky, with beautiful views to take in on either side. As you continue up the trail you'll see a wooden fence off to your right and a bench. This is the viewing spot for the giant limber pine—actually multiple trees that have grown together! The trail is mostly downhill after that, with one short uphill section. You will get a great view of Bear Lake and continue back to your car to finish the loop. Consider staying nearby at Sunrise Campground.

# SCAVENGER HUNT

### Ancient limber pine
About halfway through your hike, you'll come across the main attraction, a large limber pine. While this evergreen (doesn't lose its leaves) tree may look like one giant oddly shaped tree, it's actually five separate trees that have grown together. Scientists believe that these trees have been growing like this for 560 years!

*Pinus flexilis* ("flexible" in Latin)

### Oregon boxleaf
This is an evergreen plant, which means it holds onto its glossy and jagged-edge leaves through the winter. This makes Oregon boxleaf a good food source for animals like elk and moose in the frozen months, when other foods are limited. Can you think of any other plants that stay green in the winter?

*Paxistima myrsinites*

### Quaking aspen

This white-barked deciduous (loses its leaves) tree stands out against the evergreen trees on the trail, especially in fall. Quaking aspen leaves turn bright yellow and fall as the temperatures begin to drop. You may notice that some of the aspens are bent at odd angles. Any idea why that is? Hint: This trail gets a lot of snow in the winter.

*Populus tremuloides* (derived from the Latin word for "trembling"—notice the leaves in the wind)

### Clark's nutcracker

This crow uses its pointy beak to pick the seeds out of limber pine cones. The birds eat some immediately, but they bury most of the seeds. They return and dig them up later, but any seeds the birds might forget are left to grow into more limber pines. If you had to hide your snack to return and eat later, where would you hide it?

*Nucifraga columbiana* (Named after Lewis and Clark's voyage on the Columbia River)

### Scarlet gilia

This wildflower is also known as skyrocket because of its unique shape. Do you see a rocket ship when you look at it? Because the red flower has a long skinny body, creatures with long beaks or tongues—like humming-birds and moths—are best suited to pollinate it because they can reach way inside. Try your best to drink your water like a hummingbird at your next power-up stop.

*Ipomopsis aggregata* (means "to flock together" in Latin for its clustered tubes)

# 2

# BUNDLE UP IN ICEBOX CANYON

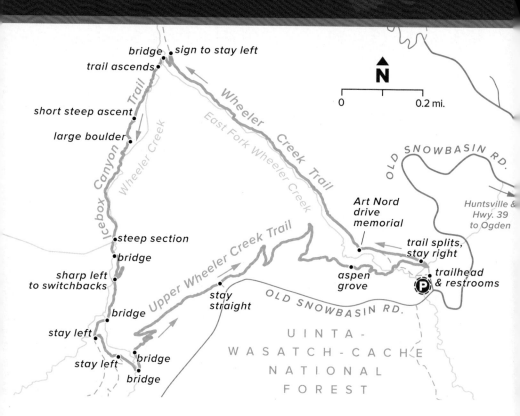

## YOUR ADVENTURE

Adventurers, today you're exploring two canyons on the historical homelands of the Eastern Shoshone, on a triangle-shaped loop that starts and
ends at the parking lot. Begin hiking to your right on the first side of the
triangle on the wide Wheeler Creek Trail, which slowly descends into the
canyon, passing the Art Nord memorial on your left. At the Icebox Canyon

In fall, this trail is remarkable for its colorful foliage →

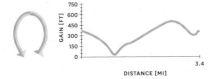

**LENGTH** 3.4-mile counterclockwise loop

**ELEVATION GAIN** 535 ft.

**HIKE + EXPLORE** 3 hours

**DIFFICULTY** Challenging—a longer trek with decent elevation gain means you'll want to power up often, and with the exposed ravine on one side you may want to hold smaller hands

**SEASON** Year-round. Fall is beautiful, as many of the leaves are changing colors. When it's particularly rainy (sometimes in the spring), avoid because it gets extremely muddy and deep footprints can damage the trail. Summer is hot, but the trail is shady once you get to the Icebox Canyon section. In winter the trail is technically open, but it can get very icy, so either avoid or bring traction (snowshoes or spikes).

**GET THERE** From I-15N in Salt Lake City, take Exit 324 for US-89N toward South Ogden. After 11 miles, take the I-84E ramp to Morgan. Drive for 4.3 miles and take Exit 92 for UT-167. Turn left onto UT-167N. Turn right to stay on UT-167. After 1.5 miles, turn left to stay on UT-167. Drive for 9.5 miles and then turn left onto UT-39W. After 1 mile, turn left onto UT-226E. Drive for 4 miles then turn right onto Ard and Nord Drive. Trailhead is straight ahead at the end of the road.

Google Maps: bit.ly/timbericebox

**RESTROOMS** Yes

**FEE** None

**TREAT YOURSELF** Stop by Chris' over in Huntsville for a thick milkshake, burger, and fries!

Uinta-Wasatch-Cache National Forest
(801) 999-2103
Facebook @USFSUWCNF

sign, turn left onto Icebox Canyon Trail. The descent will get a bit steeper just before you reach a bridge. Cross over and you'll be hiking alongside Wheeler Creek. Icebox Canyon gets its name because of how cold it stays along this stretch of the trail! Any guesses why it is so much cooler than the surrounding land? The trail remains mainly flat, but there are a few short, steep sections up. After a sharp turn left, go uphill and out of the canyon, powering up at another bridge if you need it. As you hike out, stay alert and watch for splits in the trail—stay left at the next two junctions. The trail will eventually open up and be much more sunny as you cross one more bridge. After a few switchbacks, you'll have a view of the parking lot again—stay left at this last junction and walk through a patch of aspen trees as you arrive back at the trailhead. Consider camping at Anderson Cove Campground.

# SCAVENGER HUNT

### Bigtooth maple

This deciduous (loses its leaves) tree has bright green leaves in the summer. But as soon as the cool weather hits, the leaves turn to a bright, beautiful red and orange. As they get less sunlight, there is less of the chlorophyll that makes the leaves green. Each leaf has three to five lobes or sections. Trace one and its toothy edges in your nature journal.

*Acer grandidentatum* ("big teeth" in Latin)

### Feverfew

This plant bears sunny yellow and white flowers from July to October and has feathery leaves year-round. Feverfew is a medicinal plant that acts like aspirin, and it is most commonly used as an herbal remedy to help alleviate headaches.

*Tanacetum parthenium*

### Rough horsetail

You will see this segmented plant by Wheeler Creek. Rough horsetail can usually be found next to streams, rivers, and lakes. The stalks can grow up to 3 feet tall! Is that shorter or taller than you? These rough stems have been used to deep clean pots because they contain silica (a component of sand), which makes them gritty. What do you use at your house to clean pots?

*Equisetum hyemale (equus means "horse" in Latin)*

### Common mullein

This herb can grow over 6 feet high, and it produces small yellow flowers on its tall stem in the summer. It's said that Roman soldiers used to dip the plant stalks in grease to use as torches. Today people use mullein flowers as an herbal remedy to help treat illnesses like cough, pneumonia, and flu. What do you take when you are sick?

*Verbascum thapsus*

### Black-billed magpie

This black, white, and blue songbird has a tail as long as its body! The black-billed magpie is noisy, so even if you don't catch sight of it, keep your ears open for its songs (a harsh yip) and calls (a raspy chatter). Songs are longer and complex and are used for claiming territory or finding a mate, and calls are more of a way of keeping in touch with their friends. Give your own version of a magpie song versus a call.

*Pica hudsonia*

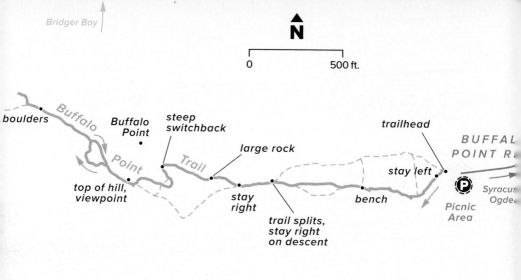

# BOUND TO THE TOP OF BUFFALO POINT

Bridger Bay

**N**

0    500 ft.

boulders

Buffalo

Buffalo
Point

steep
switchback

trailhead

BUFFAL
POINT R

large rock

Point    Trail

stay left

top of hill,
viewpoint

stay
right

bench

Syracus
Ogde

trail splits,
stay right
on descent

P

Picnic
Area

ANTELOPE ISLAND
STATE PARK

White Rock Bay

## YOUR ADVENTURE

Welcome to the historical homelands of the Fremont and Ute, adventurers.
Are you ready for a challenge? While this hike is short, you will have to
work hard to get to the top. Don't worry, though, there are plenty of benches
on the way up to power up on! There are two different paths to choose at
the beginning. Let's take the left one because it's a little wider and easier

Buffalo Point is a perfect spot to watch the sunset over the Great Salt Lake →

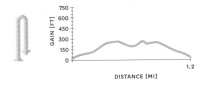

GAIN [FT]

750
600
450
300
150
0

1.2

DISTANCE [MI]

**LENGTH** 1.2-mile out and back

**ELEVATION GAIN** 285 ft.

**HIKE + EXPLORE** 1.5 hours

**DIFFICULTY** Moderate—a short hike that gains elevation quickly

**SEASON** Year-round. Best in early spring (March) and August to October, as late spring and summer bring bugs like biting gnats.

**GET THERE** From Salt Lake City, follow I-15N to UT-127/Antelope Drive in Layton. Take Exit 332 and turn west onto UT-127/Antelope Drive. Continue on Antelope Drive for 6.8 miles to the Antelope Island toll booth—after paying the fee, continue driving 8 miles to the parking lot marked for Buffalo Point.

Google Maps: bit.ly/timberbuffalopoint

**RESTROOMS** Yes

**FEE** $15

**TREAT YOURSELF** Just 2 miles north in Syracuse is Island Buffalo Grill. Get a hand-scooped root beer float!

Antelope Island State Park
(801) 725-9263
Facebook @AntelopeIslandSP

to hike up. Before long, the trail opens up and you'll have an awesome view of the Great Salt Lake to your left. Take a minute to power up on a bench and enjoy the scenery. You'll pass two more benches and reach a fork—stay left here. As you continue up the trail, it gets a bit narrower, with large rocks on either side. Before you reach the top, there's one quick but steep switchback. Use this final bench if you need it and then push on—you'll be at the top with an incredible view of the Great Salt Lake. Go right to reach Buffalo Point, but take as much time as you want exploring up top. The trail weaves through large boulders that are great for climbing. Once you're done exploring, head back the way you came. The trail splits about halfway down; while both trails lead to the parking lot, stay right (the way you came) as the trail on the left is a bit narrower and steeper. When you're done, consider camping at Bridger Bay Campground down the road.

# SCAVENGER HUNT

## American bison

This animal is the largest in North America, and it's the country's national mammal. Bison were brought to Antelope Island in 1893, and between 500

and 700 still roam freely here in a herd, eating grass as they go. If you come across one, be sure to keep your distance and slowly back away if it notices you. If you don't happen to see one while on the trail, keep an eye out while you're driving to and from your hike.

*Bison bison*

## Prairie sunflower

These beautiful yellow flowers grow in sandy, dry grasslands and bloom in the summer months. Like all sunflowers, their blooms track the movement of the sun across the sky each day.

*Helianthus petiolaris (helios means "sun" in Greek)*

## Tintic quartzite

This metamorphic rock started out as some other type of rock, but over time has been changed by high heat, high pressure, or hot mineral-rich fluids. Because Antelope Island is surrounded by the Great Salt Lake, which is full of salt and minerals, it's likely the water altered the rock. Over millions of years, grains of sand were cemented together, forming the light pink and white quartzite you see today.

Try to squish together pieces of your snack to create a "metamorphic rock" at lunchtime.

## The Great Salt Lake

Migrating birds love to stop here and snack on brine shrimp and flies in the water. Though it's not a lake you would want to dunk your head in, you actually could float in it more easily than a backyard pool because of all the salt in the water!

The largest lake west of the Mississippi River

## American avocet

Antelope Island is one of the top spots for birdwatching in all of Utah. This shorebird is one of many species that stop by during their migration. In summer, this long-legged wading bird has a black-and-white body and a rusty head and neck. Avocets build their nests directly on the ground instead of in a tree! Pretend to be an avocet: create a "nest" with rocks and twigs around you and try sitting on it (be sure to put them back when you're done).

*Recurvirostra americana*

# 4

# FROLIC IN THE FOOTHILLS OF THE WILD ROSE TRAIL

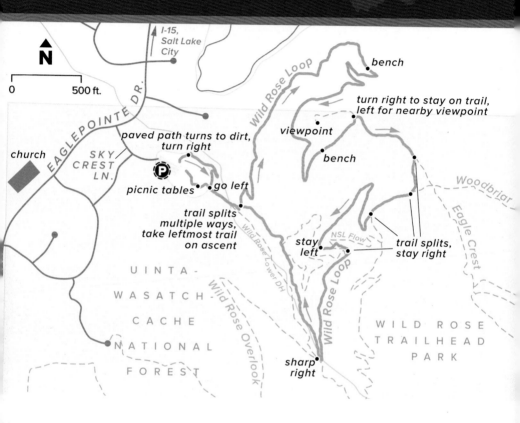

**N**

0     500 ft.

I-15, Salt Lake City

Wild Rose Loop

bench

turn right to stay on trail, left for nearby viewpoint

EAGLEPOINTE DR.

paved path turns to dirt, turn right

viewpoint

church

SKY CREST LN.

bench

picnic tables

go left

Woodbriar

trail splits multiple ways, take leftmost trail on ascent

Wild Rose Tower DH

stay left

NSL Flow

trail splits, stay right

Eagle Crest

UINTA-

WASATCH

CACHE

Wild Rose Overlook

Wild Rose Loop

WILD   ROSE

NATIONAL

TRAILHEAD

FOREST

sharp right

PARK

## YOUR ADVENTURE

Adventurers, today you're on the historical homelands of the Eastern Sho-shone. The trail starts right at the parking lot as a paved path, which quickly turns right and into dirt. Make your way through maple trees and you will emerge on grassy fields. This is where you start and end the loop. These foothills have a lot of trails throughout them, so be sure to pay attention and

This trail winds through grassy foothills →

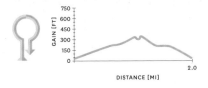

**LENGTH** 2.0-mile lollipop loop

**ELEVATION GAIN** 354 ft.

**HIKE + EXPLORE** 1.5 hours; longer to include trailhead playground

**DIFFICULTY** Moderate—gradual elevation gain

**SEASON** Year-round. Need snowshoes or spikes in winter. This is a great hike to do in the spring for all the wildflowers; because of its elevation and angle, the trail is not as muddy in spring as a lot of other Utah trails. Summer is sunny and hot, so bring protection, plenty of water, and avoid midday.

**GET THERE** From I-15N, take Exit 312 toward US-89N. Drive for 0.4 mile and merge onto Beck Street. After 1.2 miles, turn right onto Eagle Ridge Drive. At the traffic circle, continue straight for 1.6 miles. Turn right onto Eaglepointe Drive. After 0.3 mile, turn left onto Sky Crest Lane and continue to the parking lot. The trailhead starts right by the bathrooms.

Google Maps: bit.ly/timberwildrose

**RESTROOMS** Yes

**FEE** None

**TREAT YOURSELF** If you're doing a morning hike, stop by Kneaders Bakery & Cafe, 4 miles north in Salt Lake City, and get the all-you-can-eat French toast served before 11 a.m. If you hike later, they offer plenty of other pastries and desserts.

City of North Salt Lake and
Uinta-Wasatch-Cache National Forest
(801) 999-2103 and (801) 335-8726
Facebook @USFSUWCNF

stay on the correct trail. Enjoy the beautiful views of the Great Salt Lake as you're going uphill. Next, you'll take the farthest left loop and begin a mild uphill climb. A few benches provide spots to power up along the way, and you will weave in and out of shade. Where the trail splits, first take a left toward Sunset Point and walk a couple hundred feet to a bench overlooking the city. This is a great spot to enjoy a snack and a view of the Great Salt Lake, Antelope Island, and planes landing at the airport. Backtrack to the split and continue hiking the loop. The rest of the trail is downhill, so just be sure to follow the signs and keep heading down. The trail will meet up with where you started the loop.

# SCAVENGER HUNT

### Donkey tail

This succulent (any plant with fleshy tissues adapted to store water) blooms pink or red flowers on the ends of the stems in the summer, so be sure to look out for those if you are hiking in the warmer months. Do *you* think the plant looks like a donkey tail? Sketch a donkey with this succulent on the end of it in your nature journal.

*Sedum morganianum* ("to sit" in Latin, as it's sitting on the ground)

### False boneset

While this plant only reaches about 3 feet in height, its roots can grow up to 17 feet deep! Its white tubular flowers provide a lot of nectar for butterflies and moths in summer and early fall. It may not be the most beautiful flower, but how would you describe its nice smell?

*Brickellia eupatorioides*

### Woods' rose

The pink flowers bloom May through July. If you are hiking during different months, you may see the large, red rose hips on the bushes. These bright fruits are eaten by birds and other wildlife, who then disperse the seeds around the area. If you find one on the ground, find the perfect spot to leave it for a bird to find and help disperse!

*Rosa woodsii*, the trail's namesake

### Bigtooth maple

While this trail is in the foothills of Salt Lake City and mostly grassy without a lot of trees, it does have pockets where bigtooth maples grow. In the summer the leaves are a vibrant green, but as the weather cools, they turn yellow, orange, and red. The seeds and flowers provide food for native birds and small mammals.

*Acer grandidentatum*

### Arrowleaf balsamroot

The bright yellow flowers of arrowleaf balsamroot show that it's part of the sunflower family. The shape of the leaves gives you a hint about how the plant got its name. Look closely at the brown disc in the middle of each flower. Can you spot the individual flowers on the disc?

*Balsamorhiza sagittata*

# 5

# CROSS THE BEAR CANYON SUSPENSION BRIDGE

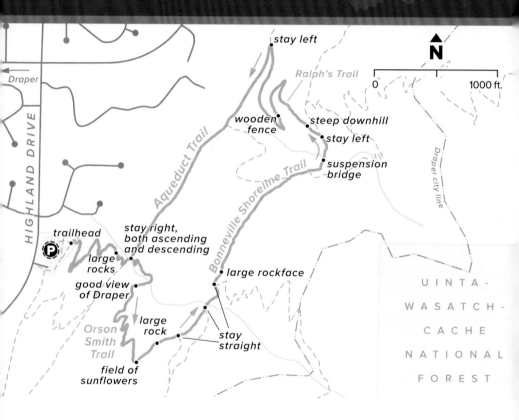

## YOUR ADVENTURE

Adventurers, let's begin on the historical homelands of the Eastern Shoshone in the foothills of the 160-mile-long Wasatch Mountain Range. The Orson Smith Trail starts right after the small playground at the park. Walk up the steps and start your uphill journey. At every corner, you get a beautiful view of the Salt Lake Valley. This is a great evening hike option to see the city

This hike is great at dusk, as Salt Lake City lights up below →

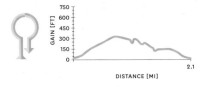

GAIN [FT]

DISTANCE [MI]

**LENGTH** 2.1-mile lollipop loop

**ELEVATION GAIN** 436 ft.

**HIKE + EXPLORE** 2.5 hours

**DIFFICULTY** Challenging—a lot of elevation gain, but beautiful views of Salt Lake County; watch the trail closely for rattlesnakes and wear close-toed shoes

**SEASON** Year-round. Great in spring and fall. Very exposed and hot in the summer, so go in the early morning or evening. Accessible in the winter with appropriate footwear (snowshoes or spikes).

**GET THERE** From I-15 in Draper, take Exit 291 for 12300 S. After about 1.5 miles, turn right on 900 E. Make a quick left onto Pioneer Road. At the roundabout, take the first exit to stay on Pioneer Road. Turn right onto Highland Drive, and after 0.3 mile, Orson Smith Park will be on your left. Park in the left parking lot closer to the playground and bathroom. Be sure to follow the posted parking signage.

Google Maps: bit.ly/timbersuspensionbridge

**RESTROOMS** Yes

**FEE** None

**TREAT YOURSELF** Stop by Crumbl Cookies, 2 miles west in Draper, after your adventure. They have new specialty flavors every week!

City of Draper
(801) 576-6500
Facebook @DraperCityUtah

light up before your eyes. At the top of the switchbacks, you'll come to a wide dirt trail full of large rocks to rest and play on. At the junction with the Aqueduct Trail, continue up the winding path that goes to the right (you'll return via the trail on the left). The switchbacks continue, and you'll be surrounded by shrubs and prairie sunflowers in the summer. There are three splits in the trail on your right—just follow the signs straight for the Bridge Loop. The trail levels out and gets a bit rocky before you come up on Bear Canyon Suspension Bridge. From there cross the bridge and follow the sign that says Bridge Loop, which takes you down to the left. The trail is a bit exposed, so stay close to the inside as you make your way back down. Take a left at the fork on the Aqueduct Trail, staying straight to get back to your first junction—go right here to head back down the switchbacks to the playground.

# SCAVENGER HUNT

### Bear Canyon suspension bridge

The Ralph L. Wadsworth Construction company built this 185-foot-long bridge without the help of any big equipment like cranes or large drills. Because the team had to travel up the mountain to build it, they brought the wood, steel beams, saws, and other tools up in pickup trucks, off-road vehicles, and a track hoe. Talk about a lot of work!

Why do you think it's called a "suspension" bridge?

### Prairie sunflower

This pollinator plant attracts bees, butterflies, and birds in the summer and fall. Its seeds come from the thousands of small flowers in the brown part of the flower. Do you like to eat sunflower seeds from the store?

*Helianthus petiolaris*

### Great Basin rattlesnake

While these reptiles can be dangerous, they usually give you a warning when they're nearby. Closely watch this trail and where you put your feet, as the snake's scales camouflage it with the surroundings. If you hear a rattle, stop and look around to find out where it's coming from. Keep a safe distance, and don't bother the snake. Their rattles are made of keratin, just like your fingernails!

*Crotalus lutosus* (*crotalus* is derived from the Greek word for "rattle")

### Rubber rabbitbrush

This type of sagebrush was used by Shoshone as a yellow dye, to make medicinal tea, and for chewing gum. It's also a great home for birds' nests and other small animals seeking cover. Take your fingers and gently rub the brush. Does it smell like rubber or pineapple to you?

*Ericameria nauseosa* ("nauseous" in Latin—how does this plant smell to you?)

### Pale evening primrose

The lovely white flowers of this plant have an especially strong fragrance. Be sure to get close and smell it. Butterflies and bees rely on pale evening primrose for their food. It's drought resistant, so it can bloom even in hot environments, opening in the early evening—hence the name! What do you like to do in the early evening?

*Oenothera pallida* ("pale" in Latin)

# 6

# DISCOVER THE HOLE AT DONUT FALLS

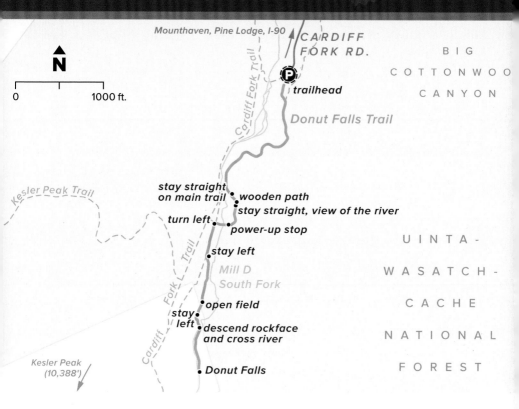

# YOUR ADVENTURE

Adventurers, let's begin on the historical homelands of the Eastern Shoshone in Big Cottonwood Canyon in the Wasatch Mountain Range. You'll have to use your navigational skills on this hike, as there are many crisscrossing trails. But as long as you follow the signs, you'll stay on target. Begin the hike up in the shade of the trees, surrounded by wildflowers in the spring and

At Donut Falls, the water flows through a round hole in the rock →

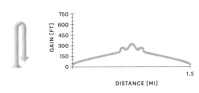

**LENGTH** 1.5 miles out and back

**ELEVATION GAIN** 308 ft.

**HIKE + EXPLORE** 1.5 hours

**DIFFICULTY** Moderate—a little elevation gain and a wide stream crossing at the end and requires a keen eye to follow the trail

**SEASON** Year-round. Spring brings high water that may not be passable. Early spring and late fall can bring snow, so be prepared. With its higher elevation and shade, summer offers a great respite from the heat of Salt Lake City. Doable in the winter with proper footwear (snowshoes or spikes), but the hike will start 1.5 miles before the trailhead when the gate is closed.

**GET THERE** From I-15 in Midvale, exit and take I-215E. Take Exit 6 for UT-190E. Turn right onto Big Cottonwood Road. After 1.7 miles, turn left onto Big Cottonwood Canyon Road. Drive up the canyon for 9 miles, then turn right on to FR019 for Donut Falls Trailhead. If it's winter, this is your parking lot. The rest of the year, continue past the gate for 0.8 mile to the Donut Falls Trailhead.

Google Maps: bit.ly/timberdonutfalls

**RESTROOMS** Yes

**FEE** None. No dogs are allowed in the canyon, or there is a fine.

**TREAT YOURSELF** Silver Fork Lodge and Restaurant has homemade hot chocolate and a nice patio.

Uinta-Wasatch-Cache National Forest
(801) 999-2103
Facebook @USFSUWCNF

summer. You'll hear the Mill D South Fork Creek running next to you most of the way. (The creeks around here were named alphabetically with letters to stand for the mills that used to be here.) Eventually you'll come across a large plank bridge, which is also a great spot to power up. When you reach a T, follow the signs to the left, then stay left at another signed junction, and pass an open field. Stay left again at a final junction, and then climb carefully down a small, jagged rock face. You'll walk along the river and then carefully cross it to view the incredible waterfall. The rock is very slippery, so be careful here and enjoy from afar. Power up while you're taking in the view, and head back the way you came. Consider making it a weekend at Jordan Pines Campground just down the road.

# SCAVENGER HUNT

### Gemmed amanita fungus

Gemmed amanita is a poisonous mushroom that can appear tan or yellow with warts on top—not very appetizing! If you find one on the ground, you can take its cap home and put it on a piece of paper with a glass over it. Come back in 24 hours to see a ring of its spores that help it reproduce!

*Amanita gemmata* ("jeweled" in Latin); make a mushroom spore print.

### Red baneberry

This plant may be fun to look at, but the berries are actually poisonous. Don't eat them! American Indians used the berries to poison the tips of their arrows. Look closely at its leaves. They are compound, which means each leaf has leaflets, and these are sharply toothed.

*Actaea rubra* ("red" in Latin)

### Bridge

This bridge is a great spot to rest and have a snack. The wooden bridge is a sturdy platform built to help keep you dry and out of the water. Salt Lake City gets 60 percent of its water from canyons in the Wasatch Mountains like this one, so the city asks people to stay out of the water to help keep it clean and sanitary.

A plank bridge crosses the Mill D North Fork Creek

### Donut Falls

This waterfall might look different from others you've seen before. The very top flows into a hole in the rock, so it's a little harder to see the whole thing. This unit of limestone is called the Donut Formation and is 330 million years old! What do you think it looked like here then?

A 100-foot cascade through a hole in the rock

### Sticky purple geranium

This beautiful pink or purple flower stands out against the surrounding greenery in the summer. The plant has the word *sticky* in its name because the flower has little hairs on it that help trap the pollen that bees carry from flower to flower. Can you see them? Play "bee tag" and pretend to hop to each flower, gathering pollen along the way.

*Geranium viscosissimum*

# 7

# FEEL THE MIST AT STEWART FALLS

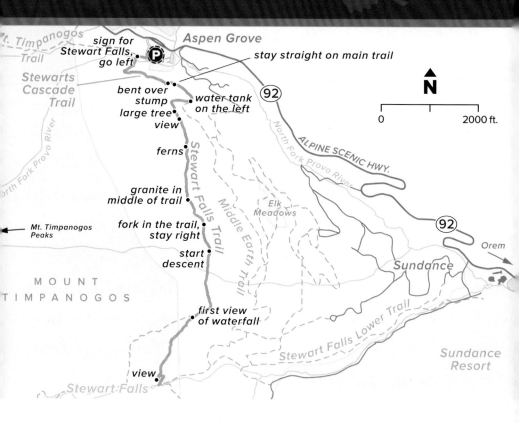

# YOUR ADVENTURE

Adventurers, today you're exploring the historical homelands of the Ute, hiking on the east side of Mount Timpanogos (11,749 feet). You'll start straight and quickly turn left at the Stewart Falls sign, crossing the North Fork Provo River on the Stewarts Cascade Trail. You'll quickly start gaining

The two-tiered Stewart Falls is more than 200 feet tall →

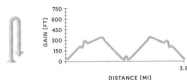

**LENGTH** 3.8 miles out and back

**ELEVATION GAIN** 656 ft.

**HIKE + EXPLORE** 3 hours

**DIFFICULTY** Challenging—wide dirt trail with lots of exposed roots, lots of ups and downs, but a fun one to snowshoe in winter; the descent from the ridge down to the base of the falls is steep

**SEASON** Year-round. Wildflowers in bloom and the waterfall has a stronger flow in the spring, hot in the summer but a good amount of shade, and can be accessed in the snowy winter with appropriate footwear (snowshoes or spikes).

**GET THERE** From I-15 in Orem, take Exit 800N. Follow 800N for 2.4 miles. Stay left and take the US-189N ramp. Drive for 7 miles. Just past Vivian Park, turn left onto UT-92W for Sundance. Drive 4.8 miles past Aspen Grove for the Stewart Falls Trailhead.

Google Maps: bit.ly/timberstewartfalls

**RESTROOMS** Yes

**FEE** $6

**TREAT YOURSELF** Grab a fresh-baked pastry from the Sundance Deli, about 3 miles south.

Uinta-Wasatch-Cache National Forest, Pleasant Grove Ranger District
(801) 785-3563
Facebook @USFSUWCNF

elevation through large pine trees surrounding the trail. Watch out for the exposed roots as you stay left on the trail past the BYU Aspen Grove Trail. You'll pass a large covered water tank and the trees will start to change from pine to aspen. Stay straight here, passing the Middle Earth side trail to your left. Avoid touching stinging nettles among the ferns along the trail. Stay right as you pass two side trails. You're getting close to the waterfall when the trail descends and then ascends again. Listen for it as you approach your first viewpoint, staying left at the trail junction. As you approach the waterfall, the trail has loose rock, so watch your step and go slowly. There's a large outcropping of rock that's a nice viewpoint. To go down to the river, make a sharp left on the trail—no need to scale the rocks. Enjoy a nice lunch as you watch the waterfall and its cool mist. Just remember, you will now have to hike back up. So power up and get ready for a fun challenge the way you came! Camping is available at the Mount Timpanogos Campground near the trailhead.

## SCAVENGER HUNT

### Stewart Falls

Stewart Falls is created from runoff of the glacier on Mount Timpanogos. With an upper and lower tier, it is more than 200 feet tall and has the most water in early spring.

Named after the family who homesteaded in the area

### Rock slab

Perhaps granite or limestone, this is the perfect spot to sit on if you need a break—or to slide down. How do you think it found its way to the center of the trail? Granite is a tough stone—you may have even eaten off a granite countertop!

Igneous rock (formed by cooling magma)

### Western bracken fern

These nonflowering plants have been on Earth for around 360 million years! Dinosaurs used to eat them. There are hundreds of different species of ferns, and its tiny spores have helped this fern spread around the world. Can you identify its triangular frond (the whole branch) and see the even smaller pinnules (subleaflets)?

*Pteridium aquilinum* ("eagle" in Latin—Carl Linnaeus, who gave it this name, thought its roots resembled an eagle)

### Quaking aspen

These deciduous (loses its leaves) trees grow year-round, even in the harsh winter! They provide food and nourishment for lots of animals in every season. Some of these animals include moose, black bear, beaver, porcupine, and rodents. The trees contain a green, sugary layer underneath their white bark. With a piece of paper and pencil, make a bark rubbing of aspen and label it in your nature journal.

*Populus tremuloides* (derived from the Latin word for "trembling")

### Moose

This ungulate is one of the largest species in the world. An adult male can weigh up to 1800 pounds! If you spot one, make sure you keep a safe distance and don't disturb it. If they're far off the trail, calmly walk by. If you see one on the trail, wait to see if it will move along. If not, try to find an alternative route—or simply turn around.

*Alces alces*, an ungulate is a mammal with hooves

# 8

# SPOT THE ROCK CLIMBERS AT MAPLE CANYON ARCH

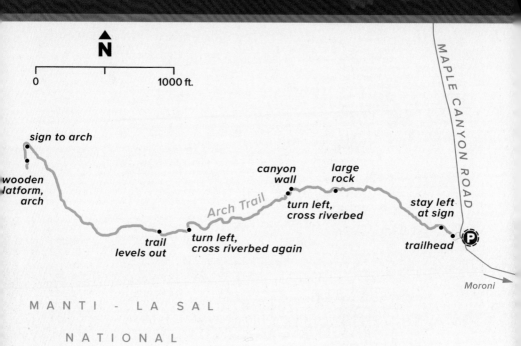

## YOUR ADVENTURE

Adventurers, today you're on the historical homelands of the Ute. The trail starts on the left side of the road as you're driving up. A sign at the trailhead points you to the arch; take your first left toward the arch and pass a picnic table. Keep an eye out for rock climbers—they love this canyon! Follow the trail right up to the canyon wall. Don't hike along the wall, though; follow

Fall offers a colorful view of Maple Canyon Arch →

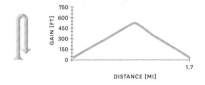

**LENGTH** 1.7 miles out and back

**ELEVATION GAIN** 551 ft.

**HIKE + EXPLORE** 2 hours

**DIFFICULTY** Moderate—trail winds through the canyon, with some steep uphill sections; levels out before getting to the arch

**SEASON** Year-round. Great fall foliage with the maples; in winter will need appropriate footwear (snowshoes or spikes).

**GET THERE** From I-15S, take Exit 225 for UT-132. Turn left and drive for 14 miles. Turn right onto W 400 S. After 0.5 mile, turn left. Drive for 5.6 miles and turn right onto S Freedom Road. Drive for 0.5 mile, and then turn right onto Maple Canyon Road. After 3 miles, the trailhead will be on your left.

Google Maps: bit.ly/timbermaplecanyon

**RESTROOMS** Yes

**FEE** $5

**TREAT YOURSELF** After your hike stop by Shalan's, 10 miles east in Moroni, and enjoy a tasty ice cream or specialty soda.

Manti-La Sal National Forest
(435) 636-3500
Facebook @MantiLaSalNationalForest

the trail across the riverbed. About a half mile into the hike the trail gets a bit steep. Power up, push through, and you'll find it levels out before you get to the arch. Turn left and cross the riverbed again and you'll soon come to a large sign telling you to go left for the arch. You'll quickly come to a wooden platform. Look up to get a good view! There is a little cave and a slot canyon behind the arch you can explore if you're up for a longer adventure. When you're done exploring, turn around and follow your steps back to your car. When you're done, consider making it a weekend at Maple Canyon Campground right at the trailhead.

# SCAVENGER HUNT

### Bigtooth maple

While most of northern Utah is covered in pine trees and aspens, you might guess that Maple Canyon is full of maple trees—specifically bigtooth maples. In the spring, look for the tree's seedpods, double-sided samaras with wings that help them disperse in the wind near and far. If you find one on the ground, give it a spin. Race your samaras with a hiking buddy.

*Acer grandidentatum*

### Oregon boxleaf

See if you can count how many of the lance-shaped leaves are on one branch of this evergreen plant. In the spring, you can see their tiny maroon flowers. How many of those can you see?

*Paxistima myrsinites*

## Conglomerate rock

Do you wonder how all those large rocks got stuck in the walls of the canyon? This is called conglomerate, and it's a sedimentary rock made of rounded rocks and sand that are usually cemented together by lime carbonate or iron oxides. They come together when water transports them to a basin, where the rocks get trapped. Try crushing two different cookies together and adding some water to it to create your own conglomerate cookie.

This sedimentary rock is around 100 million years old and is found all along the canyon.

## Rock climbers

Maple Canyon's walls are one of the top locations for rock climbing in the world! Hundreds of climbers come here every week. Have you ever tried rock climbing before? Keep your eyes peeled, and you'll be sure to see someone with a rope attached to them scaling the large conglomerate rock walls.

Hailey's mom, Jo, rock climbing in Maple Canyon

## Mule deer

These mammals get their name because of their long, mule-like ears. They eat broad-leafed plants like maples and Oregon boxleaf that you've seen along this trail. Be sure not to approach or feed deer if you do happen to catch a glimpse of them. It's important for deer to find food on their own so they eat appropriate wild foods. Only the males grow antlers.

*Odocoileus hemionus*

# 9

# SOAK IN THE FIFTH WATER HOT SPRINGS

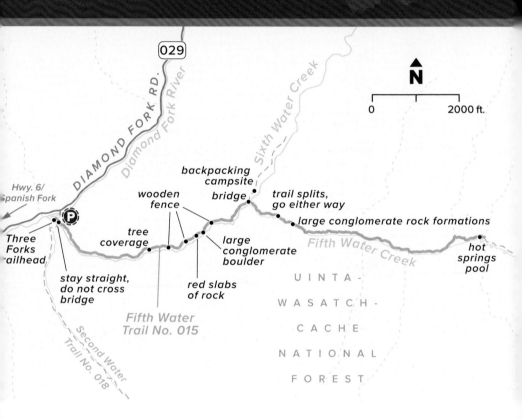

029

DIAMOND FORK RD.

Diamond Fork River

Sixth Water Creek

N

0          2000 ft.

Hwy. 6/
Spanish Fork

backpacking
campsite

wooden
fence

bridge

trail splits,
go either way

large conglomerate rock formations

Three
Forks
Trailhead

tree
coverage

large
conglomerate
boulder

Fifth Water Creek

hot
springs
pool

stay straight,
do not cross
bridge

red slabs
of rock

UINTA-

Fifth Water
Trail No. 015

WASATCH-

CACHE

Second Water
Trail No. 018

NATIONAL

FOREST

## YOUR ADVENTURE

Adventurers, today you're on the historical homelands of the Ute. The Fifth Water Trail starts as you walk through a cattle gate. There is a bridge off to the right, but don't cross it—follow the trail straight. You'll be following Fifth Water Creek for the first half, so it's an easy trail to navigate. As you wind through the canyon, notice all the different trees and rock formations. At the

Fifth Water Hot Springs is a hidden gem tucked in Diamond Fork Canyon →

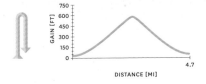

**LENGTH** 4.7 miles out and back

**ELEVATION GAIN** 607 ft.

**HIKE + EXPLORE** 3–4 hours, depending on how long you spend at the hot springs

**DIFFICULTY** Challenging—a decent amount of elevation gain and longer for little legs

**SEASON** Best in spring and fall: Spring has great wildflowers (but can get slippery after a rain) and fall offers beautiful maple foliage. Summer can get really hot (even the hot springs get too hot), and the gate is closed in winter (November–May), making the hike almost 8 miles.

**GET THERE** From I-15S, take the US-6E exit toward Price. Keep left and follow signs for US-6E/Price. Drive for 11 miles and then turn left onto Diamond Fork Road. After about 10 miles, you'll come to the trailhead on the right. Limited parking

Google Maps: bit.ly/timberfifthwaterhotsprings

**RESTROOMS** Yes

**FEE** None

**TREAT YOURSELF** Stop at the Little Acorn, 16 miles east at the mouth of Spanish Fork Canyon. They have grilled cheese on homemade bread and delicious shakes.

Uinta-Wasatch-Cache National Forest
(801) 999-2103
Facebook @USFSUWCNF

halfway point you'll cross a bridge to the right—this is also an area where you can camp if you feel like packing in all your gear! Continue following the trail until it splits; both directions meet up again after a few hundred feet, so you can choose either, but the lower trail is a little more washed out, narrow, and exposed. When you start to smell the sulfur of the hot spring, you'll know you're close. (Be forewarned: There may be nude bathers in the hot spring and on the trail.) Choose any of the little pools to soak in: There are upper and lower springs. The higher up you go, the warmer the water gets. When you're done splashing, follow your steps back the way you came.

# SCAVENGER HUNT

### Tree swallow

Like many birds, male and female tree swallows are different colors. The males have a bright blue-green back, while the females are a little duller blue with more brown. Tree swallows like to live near water, making this canyon along the river a perfect habitat for them. Would you like to live near the water?

*Tachycineta bicolor*

### Conglomerate rock

Do you notice that some of the walls and large boulders have a bunch of river rocks sticking out of them? The rock is called conglomerate, a sedimentary rock made of rounded rocks and sand that are usually cemented together by lime carbonate or iron oxides. See how many individual pieces of rock you can count in 60 seconds!

Large conglomerate rock slab

### Juniper

Though you'll probably see plenty of maple trees on the trail, keep an eye out for juniper trees too. Junipers only grow to about 30 feet and may have blue cones that look like purple berries on their branches. They aren't good to eat raw, but the berries do have a peppery taste and have been used in rubs and sauces. The Ute made medicine from the leaves to help treat vomiting, arthritis, and coughing.

*Juniperus* sp.

### Hoary tansyaster

These small purple flowers are part of the daisy family. Do you see any resemblance to the daisies you're used to seeing? These flowers help support biodiversity—a variety of wildlife. They are a popular flower with bees and other pollinators. See if you can sit and watch one for five minutes and count how many things come by to pollinate them.

*Machaeranthera canescens*

### Fifth Water Hot Springs

The water in a hot spring is warm because of geothermal heat—warmth from magma under the Earth's surface heats nearby rock! The temperature of each little pool varies depending on how deep it is and how close to the source of the spring it is. The eggy smell you'll probably notice comes from a high concentration of the element sulfur in the water.

How far away from the pool you are in do you think the heat source is?

# 10

# BOARDWALK YOUR WAY AROUND MIRROR LAKE

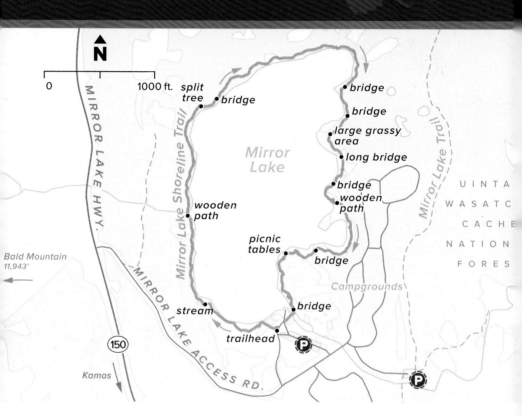

## YOUR ADVENTURE

Adventurers, let's begin on the historical homelands of the Eastern Shoshone in the Uinta Mountains, with many peaks over 12,000 feet, including Utah's highest (King's Peak; 13,528'). It's one of the only mountain ranges in the United States that runs east to west. Let's start going clockwise, taking the Mirror Lake Shoreline Trail to the left. Many boardwalks will help your

The trail follows the shoreline around 36-foot deep Mirror Lake →

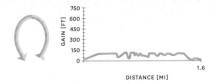

GAIN [FT]

750
600
450
300
150
0

1.6

DISTANCE [MI]

**LENGTH** 1.6-mile loop

**ELEVATION GAIN** 39 ft.

**HIKE + EXPLORE** 1.5 hours

**DIFFICULTY** Easy—a flat trail with lots of fun places to stop and play. High elevation, so may get out of breath.

**SEASON** Late June to October; road closes in winter with the first snow, so be sure to check with rangers. Late spring can be muddy but has wildflowers; summer is lush and green, and early fall has colorful foliage.

**GET THERE** From I-15 in Salt Lake City, take I-80E. Take Exit 146 toward Heber. Take Exit 4 toward UT-248E. After 11 miles, turn left onto S Main Street. Turn right onto Center Street/Highway 150 and drive for 31 miles. Turn right onto Forest Rd 104. Turn left to stay on Forest Rd 104.

Google Maps: bit.ly/timbermirrorlakeloop

**RESTROOMS** Yes

**FEE** $6

**TREAT YOURSELF** Try the famous milkshakes from Hi-Mountain in Kamas, 32 miles west toward town.

Uinta-Wasatch-Cache National Forest
Heber-Kamas Ranger District
(801) 999-2103
Facebook @USFSUWCNF

feet stay dry, but be sure to take a look over the edges to see what is below your feet—the little streams and puddles under the boardwalks contain some exciting wildlife! Pass a shoreside spot to power up and play at along the lake's edge. You may see some people sitting on the edge of the lake and fishing. If you hang around long enough, you might just be lucky enough to watch someone reel one in. The trail is bordered by lots of pine trees and big rocks that are fun to climb. Continue making your way around the lake, crossing bridges and enjoying the calm water just a few strides away. Toward the end of your hike (on the southeastern side of the lake), there are some picnic tables that would make a great spot to stop for lunch. Consider camping right there by the lake at Mirror Lake Campground.

## SCAVENGER HUNT

### Elk

If you see an elk with antlers, it's a male. Their antlers are made of bone and can grow as fast as 1 inch per day! How fast do your bones grow? Not only are elk fast at growing antlers, they also are fast runners. A grown bull can run as quickly as 40 miles per hour—as fast as a car!

*Cervus canadensis*

### Pine marten

You might spot one of these cute mammals in a tree. Part of the weasel family, they have a long body with round ears. Pine martens eat smaller animals like mice and chipmunks as well as berries and insects. They have fierce claws to climb trees. Look at your fingernails—do you think you would be as good a climber as a marten?

*Martes americana*

### Rainbow trout

These fish are easy to identify because they are shiny and spotted, with an iridescent pink stripe along their side. They all come from the Kamas

State Fish Hatchery, which has been raising fish since 1930 to be stocked in these lakes! Write a story in your nature journal about the journey of a fish from the hatchery to this lake. How did it get here?

*Oncorhynchus mykiss*

### Hoary comma butterfly

This beautiful insect is commonly seen throughout North America. The hoary comma, which is about 2 inches across, is easy to identify because its

wings have a distinctive ragged edge. It feeds on sap from trees and nectar from flowers. Sketch this beauty in your nature journal, and try to color its orange and black markings when you get home.

*Polygonia gracilis*

### Boardwalk

This 53-acre lake's edges feature lots of little streams and marshy areas. Boardwalks were built to keep your feet dry and off the fragile ecosystem at ground level. Can you count how many boardwalks you cross as you hike around the whole lake? Stop to look over the edges now and then to see what's underneath. You'll be surprised how much you're walking right over!

A boardwalk around Mirror Lake

# 11

# FOLLOW THE DINOSAUR TRACKS AT RED FLEET STATE PARK

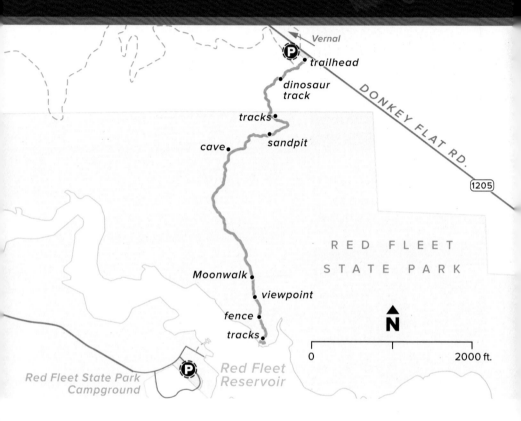

## YOUR ADVENTURE

Adventurers, today you're on the historical homelands of the Ute in the south range of the Uinta Mountains. You'll begin among the swirly red rocks of the Nugget Sandstone Formation. Begin on a part-sand, part-rock hop trail, looking carefully for the painted-in dinosaur tracks and signs leading all the way to the end, at the water. You'll begin on sand and slowly climb up

Follow these tracks to the end of the trail, where you will see hundreds more! →

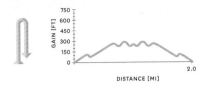

750
600
450
300
150
0

GAIN [FT]

2.0

DISTANCE [MI]

**LENGTH** 2.0 miles out and back

**ELEVATION GAIN** 272 ft.

**HIKE + EXPLORE** 2.5 hours

**DIFFICULTY** Challenging—marked trail is helpful and it's fairly short for the rewards, but you'll need to walk over sand and uneven rocks most of the way

**SEASON** Year-round. Late summer, fall, and early spring have the most exposed dinosaur tracks, and fall has beautiful yellow aspens.

**GET THERE** From Vernal, take US-191N for 7.8 miles and turn right onto Donkey Flat Road. The parking lot will be on your right in 2.4 miles.

Google Maps: bit.ly/timberdinotracks

**RESTROOMS** Yes

**FEE** None

**TREAT YOURSELF** Freddy's Frozen Custard & Steakburgers in Vernal has a create-your-own sundae bar.

Red Fleet State Park
(435) 789-4432
Facebook @RedFleetStatePark

some of the rock. Be sure to power up in the shade along the way. Soon, on your right, you'll see a small cave up high in the rock. What do you think it looks like inside? Walk past a prickly pear patch and begin crossing larger outcroppings of rock. Finally, you'll approach a fence with signs indicating more dinosaur tracks. You'll head downhill toward the water and come upon three placards—look very closely and see if you can find 1, 5, or maybe even 300 tracks! When you're done, head back the way you came. Consider extending the adventure by camping at Red Fleet Campground on the reservoir.

# SCAVENGER HUNT

### Dinosaur track

Can you imagine these three-toed dinosaurs marching around here on former river-beds, 157 million years ago? Look for one of several hundred prints between here and the reservoir. A series of three or more prints from the same animal is considered to be a trackway. Sketch them in your journal and compare the size of their feet to yours. Which is bigger?

An artist's rendering of *Dilophosaurus wetherilli;* a *Dilophosaurus* (two-crested lizard) track

### Plains prickly pear cactus

Look for these spiny succulents (plants that hold water) whose pink fruits look like pears. The spines on each pad are actually modified leaves! You'll see yellow, orange, or magenta flowers in the late spring and early summer. Cacti can live in the dry desert because their stems plump up with water whenever it rains, allowing them to save the water for later. Do the prickly pear leaf pads look full of water or dried up today?

*Opuntia polyacantha* ("many thorns" in Latin)

### Red rocks

These are red buttes—tall, flat-topped towers of rock. The lower portions are part of the Chinle Formation, deposited 225 million years ago, and the upper parts are made of Nugget Sandstone, formed from sand dunes between 180 and 210 million years ago! Sketch them in your journal, and who might climb them.

Do you see the ships?

### Utah juniper

Look closely at the bark of this tree. American Indians traditionally peeled it and wove it into sleeping mats and sandals. You may find critters nearby enjoying their blue cones, which look like berries. Juniper berries have a waxy coating that protects the seed inside from losing moisture in this harsh environment. Utah juniper trees can live to be 1000 years old! How old do you think this one is?

*Juniperus osteosperma*

### Cave

How do you think the process of erosion makes caves like this one? Imagine water dripping slowly into this sandstone. Could water make a shape like you see? How long do you think it would take to erode a cave like this?

A small cave in the sandstone wall

# 12

# LOOK ACROSS LANDSCAPE ARCH

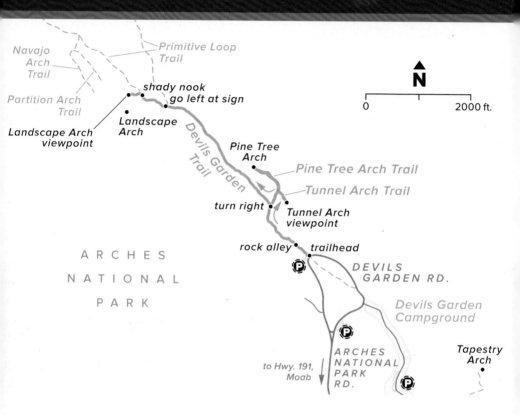

Navajo Arch Trail

Primitive Loop Trail

shady nook
go left at sign

Partition Arch Trail

Landscape Arch viewpoint

Landscape Arch

Devils Garden Trail

Pine Tree Arch

Pine Tree Arch Trail

Tunnel Arch Trail

turn right

Tunnel Arch viewpoint

rock alley

trailhead

A R C H E S

N A T I O N A L

P A R K

DEVILS GARDEN RD.

Devils Garden Campground

to Hwy. 191, Moab

ARCHES NATIONAL PARK RD.

Tapestry Arch

N

0        2000 ft.

## YOUR ADVENTURE

Adventurers, today you're on the historical homelands of the Ute. You'll begin walking on the Devils Garden Trail in the northern area of the park between two tall rock walls and then start to gradually go uphill. Your first stop is to the right, when you'll take the side trail to Tunnel Arch, and then back the other way to see the unique Pine Tree Arch. Head back to the main trail and

How much longer do you think Landscape Arch will last? →

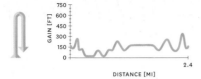

**LENGTH** 2.4 miles out and back

**ELEVATION GAIN** 308 ft.

**HIKE + EXPLORE** 2.5 hours

**DIFFICULTY** Easy—rollercoaster up and down on a wide gravel trail with just one sandy spot

**SEASON** Year-round. Trail is exposed to sun, so be sure to bring water and sunscreen and attempt to go in the morning or late afternoon for less intense rays.

**GET THERE** From Moab, take US-191 north for 4 miles to the Arches National Park entrance on your right. The park is very popular, so try to show up early as they close the entry mid-morning every day and only open it back up after the congestion clears. From the entrance station, drive 17.5 miles on Main Park Road to the Devils Garden parking lot. The trailhead is in the middle of the parking lot. Extend the fun and camp at Devils Garden Campground nearby.

Google Maps: bit.ly/timberlandscape

**RESTROOMS** Yes

**FEE** $30. The park is piloting a timed entry system from April to October, and you'll need to go to recreation.gov and purchase an hour time slot for $2. They release some the day before for last-minute planners.

**TREAT YOURSELF** MOYO (Moab Frozen Yogurt) is just 5 miles south of the Arches entrance. Try a homemade ice cream sandwich!

Arches National Park
(435) 719-2299
Facebook @ArchesNPS

keep going up and down, passing cool rock formations all the way. Soon you'll reach a sign—go left first to the Landscape Arch viewpoint. You'll walk through a small sand pit, and then head all the way to the end of the deck to look straight up to Landscape Arch. When you're done admiring it, head back the way you came and consider camping at Devils Garden Campground. The trail continues onward to Navajo, Partition, and Double O Arches, so if your fellow hikers aren't too beat, consider going all the way! Don't forget to grab your stamp and Junior Ranger badge at the visitor center when you're done.

# SCAVENGER HUNT

### Tunnel Arch

Arches National Park has the densest concentration of stone arches in the world—more than 2000! First, fins of rock like this one form holes known as windows, and these are rounded out by sand grains suspended in the wind. To be officially called an arch, the rock's hole must be at least 3 feet in diameter and be connected to the base, like a door frame. How big do you think Tunnel Arch's hole is?

This formation looks like a tunnel passing through the sandstone fin

### Pine Tree Arch

Most of the arches in the park are made from Entrada Sandstone, a sedimentary rock layer that is over 160 million years old. This place used to be a massive desert full of sand dunes. Over time, the dunes formed this rock that is very porous (full of tiny holes), which allows water to trickle in. Stand underneath this arch right next to the pine tree and do your best pine tree imitation.

Pine Tree Arch

## Microbiotic soil

Look for something that resembles black frosting on the ground off the trail. It looks dry, but there is a hidden world of life! Microscopic fungi, bacteria, lichens, mosses, and other life forms all inhabit this special soil that makes plant life in the water-starved desert possible. Be careful not to disturb it, but imagine zooming in with your eyes like a microscope and sketch what might be happening inside this special dirt.

Microbiotic soil appears black and crusty

## Sacred thorn-apple

Look for these white, wide-open blossoms and their thorny green fruit like a spiky apple from May through October. The flowers of sacred thorn-apple are pollinated by moths, and they don't smell great—maybe as a warning that they're poisonous if eaten!

*Datura wrightii*

## Landscape Arch

Water has slowly shaped the arch for centuries, dissolving cement between sand grains, dripping into cracks, freezing and then expanding, causing breakages. Imagine eating your lunch here and hearing the *crack* of a 60-foot-long slab of rock falling. It happened in 1991! That's why you can no longer go directly underneath this fragile arch today.

The longest arch in the world!

# TAKE A LOOK THROUGH TURRET ARCH AND THE WINDOWS

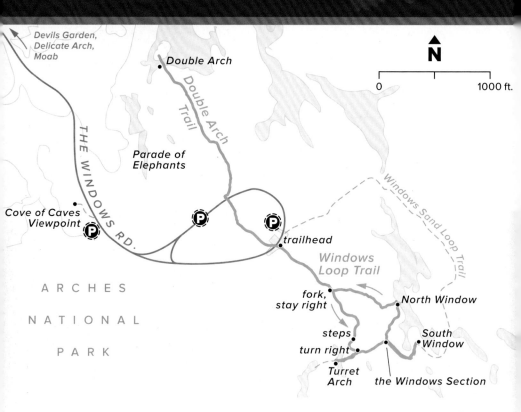

## YOUR ADVENTURE

Adventurers, today you're on the historical homelands of the Ute to explore a collection of arches known as the Windows Section. You'll head to Double Arch first. From the parking lot, take the far north trailhead—a short, straight shot to the viewpoint. Power up here under the awesomeness and continue back to the parking lot. In the middle of the parking lot, take the

Do you see the Parade of Elephants in the Windows Section? →

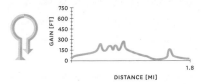

**LENGTH** 1.8-mile lollipop loop

**ELEVATION GAIN** 282 ft.

**HIKE + EXPLORE** 1.5 hours

**DIFFICULTY** Easy—wide gravel trail with some steps up to view under each arch

**SEASON** Year-round. Trail is exposed to sun, so bring lots of water and plan to visit early or late in the day in warmer months.

**GET THERE** From Moab, take US-191 north for 4 miles to the Arches National Park entrance on your right. The park is very popular, so try to show up early as they will close the entry mid-morning every day and only open it back up after the congestion clears. From the entrance station, go 9 miles on Scenic Arches Drive, and then turn right on Windows Road. Take that for 2.4 miles to the parking lot at the end. The trailhead is at the end of the parking lot. There are two trailheads, Double Arch and Windows Loop; start at the far one, Double Arch.

Google Maps: bit.ly/timberwindows

**RESTROOMS** Yes

**FEE** $30. The park is piloting a timed entry system from April to October, and you'll need to go to Recreation.gov and purchase an hour time slot for $2. They release some the day before for last-minute planners.

**TREAT YOURSELF** Sweet Cravings Moab has yummy monkey bread, scones, and more that are just begging to be put in your daypack to enjoy on the trail!

Arches National Park
(435) 719-2299
Facebook @ArchesNPS

stairs up to arrive at the Windows Loop trailhead. The huge arches loom before you as you walk closer to them—go right when you reach the fork. You'll head a little bit up and then you'll see a fork going to the right to explore Turret Arch. Carefully climb up and explore, and then head back to the trail, continuing straight. Next you'll turn right to curve around and check out the South Window. Head back to the main trail as it curves around to the North Window. You can climb up and under this massive arch as well, and head back to the trail. Find yourself back at the first fork, and continue straight back to the parking lot. Don't forget to grab your stamp and Junior Ranger badge at the visitor center when you're done, and consider camping at Devils Garden Campground for more fun.

# SCAVENGER HUNT

### Double Arch

Double Arch offers double the fun! Both arches are joined at one end. Double Arch is the third-largest, the tallest, and second-longest arch in the park. Its largest span is 144 feet by 112 feet, and the smaller opening is 67 feet by 86 feet. When you get home, use some clay to try and re-create this masterpiece.

Double Arch, formed from top-to-bottom erosion

### Turret Arch

In architecture, a turret is a small tower that projects vertically from the wall of a building like a medieval castle. It's also been called the Kneeling Camel and the Jailhouse. In your nature journal, sketch Turret Arch as a kneeling camel, a castle, and a jailhouse.

The keyhole-shaped arch is 105 feet long, 64 feet high, and 39 feet wide.

### South Window

This is a twin window in the same sandstone fin as its sister, the North

Window, creating a fun eyeglass effect in the rock. It's almost as if they were talking to each other as they formed, making sure they stayed the same size. Imagine a conversation between these two. What might they be saying?

This arch is the third largest in the park.

### North Window

At 90 feet wide and 54 feet high, how much taller is the North Window than you? Five times? Ten times? Windows aren't quite arches ... yet. Arches begin as windows, and as water and wind weather

the rock, the windows enlarge until they reach the base of the rock they're on and take the form of the other huge arches you'll see in the park today.

Views of North Window and under the arch

### Delicate Arch

Consider getting up early and making the 3.2-mile trek (with 629 feet of elevation gain) to this nearby beauty. The opening beneath the arch is 32 feet wide and 46 feet high, making it the largest free-standing arch in the park. Can you do a backbend to mimic the shape of Delicate Arch?

What do you think this arch will look like in 100 years?

# 14

# SCALE THE SLICKROCK OF WHALE ROCK

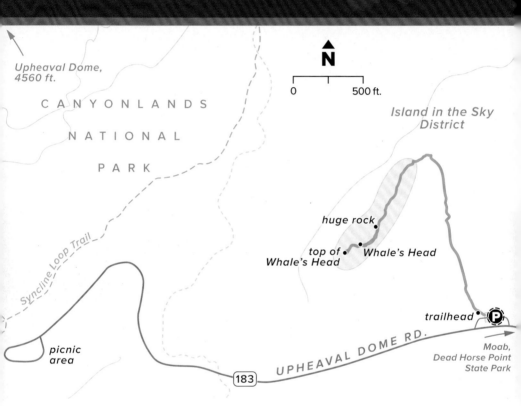

Upheaval Dome,
4560 ft.

C A N Y O N L A N D S

N A T I O N A L

P A R K

Syncline Loop Trail

N

0    500 ft.

Island in the Sky
District

huge rock

top of • Whale's Head
Whale's Head

trailhead • P

picnic
area

183    UPHEAVAL DOME RD.

Moab,
Dead Horse Point
State Park

## YOUR ADVENTURE

Adventurers, today you're on the historical homelands of the Ute. You're
exploring the top of a mesa, the Island in the Sky, at Canyonlands today.
At the trailhead, you'll see what you're going to climb: Whale Rock, made
out of soft Navajo Sandstone that eroded into this animal's shape. Your
hike begins almost immediately on the slickrock. Cairns (small rock piles)

Up, up, up you go to ride the red whale! →

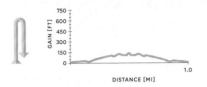

**LENGTH** 1.0 mile out and back

**ELEVATION GAIN** 112 ft.

**HIKE + EXPLORE** 1.5 hours

**DIFFICULTY** Moderate—the trail is short but is mostly rock, with a couple of somewhat steep climbs; be sure to outfit your kids in shoes with some traction—they'll be stoked to see how they "stick" to the rock

**SEASON** Year-round. Great hike for a sunset. Spring and fall offer cooler weather, late summer and early fall have thunderstorms. Completely exposed, so on warm days, be sure to go early and bring sun protection and extra water.

**GET THERE** From Moab, take US-191 north for 11 miles. Turn left onto UT-313W and drive 14.6 miles. Continue onto Island in the Sky Road for 13 miles, turn right onto Upheaval Dome Road and go 4 miles. The parking lot will be on your right.

Google Maps: bit.ly/timberwhale

**RESTROOMS** Yes

**FEE** $30 or free with annual pass

**TREAT YOURSELF** It's always Taco Tuesday at Giliberto's Mexican Taco Shop. Fuel up when you return to Moab after your adventure.

Canyonlands National Park
(435) 719-2313
Facebook @CanyonlandsNPS

will be your friend today, so appoint someone to be Lead Cairn Spotter. Don't add any here that could confuse other hikers, though! You'll head straight and then begin to curve left to climb up the tail of the whale. Climb up the head of the whale, if you dare! Play around then head back the way you came. Get your stamp and Junior Ranger badge at the visitor center, and consider camping at Dead Horse Point State Park (water available) for even more Canyonlands fun.

# SCAVENGER HUNT

### Navajo Sandstone

The top of the mesa (a flat-topped hill) and the whale formation is Navajo Sandstone. This area was a giant sea 190 million years ago! Sandstone is easily eroded into domes. Make a pile of dirt at the beginning of the trail, and blow on it to show what wind can do to particles.

These sandstone cliffs are over 1000 feet above the surrounding terrain

### Colorado pinyon pine

Look for these squat plants, seemingly growing straight out of the rock. Their crooked trunks and reddish bark are clues that they grow slowly in these harsh conditions—even the smallest ones might be 80 to 100 years old. Its roots are extensive and often mirror the size of the aboveground tree. Search for the small cones that hold pine nuts inside. Critters love to snack on these—and so do American Indians, traditionally.

*Pinus edulis*

### Cairns

A cairn is a mound of stones built as a landmark. Every park has different rules about cairns, so check out a park's website for information on hiking trails before you go. At Canyonlands, the park rangers made cairns to withstand the elements, so don't disturb these or add any of your own.

A small rock pile marks the way

### Potholes

Look for small holes along the top of the whale. Some may hold standing water. A pothole is formed when a circular current of water carrying small pebbles and sediment begins to wear away a rock surface. Are there any creatures in the potholes today?

A pothole eroded into the stone

### Upheaval Dome

This 6.2-mile-wide crater has a unique dome in the middle of it. One geological theory is that Upheaval Dome is a salt bubble; another is that it could be an impact crater from a meteorite. Which do you think is correct?

View of Upheaval Dome from the top of Whale's Head

# 15

# GAZE OUT FROM GRAND VIEW POINT

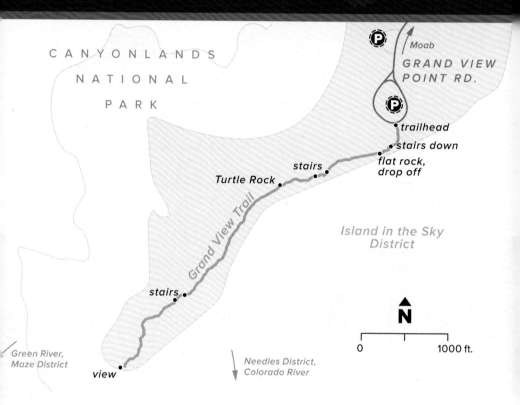

CANYONLANDS
NATIONAL
PARK

Moab

GRAND VIEW
POINT RD.

trailhead
stairs down
flat rock,
drop off

stairs
Turtle Rock
Grand View Trail

Island in the Sky
District

stairs

N

0          1000 ft.

Green River,
Maze District

view

Needles District,
Colorado River

## YOUR ADVENTURE

Adventurers, today you're on the historical homelands of the Ute. You'll
begin by heading down stone stairs to a view of White Rim Road (colored by
salt) that goes on for days. Once down, be careful of the sheer drop-offs—the
trail continues far to the right of the edge. You'll go up a few more stairs,
and then the land around you narrows. You'll truly feel like you might be on

The view from the end of the Island in the Sky is spectacular →

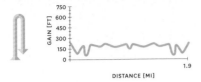

GAIN [FT]

750
600
450
300
150
0

1.9

DISTANCE [MI]

**LENGTH** 1.9 miles out and back

**ELEVATION GAIN** 197 ft.

**HIKE + EXPLORE** 1.5 hours

**DIFFICULTY** Moderate—most of the time you're walking directly on rock, with some exposed ledges (hold hands at these parts with littles)

**SEASON** Year-round. Spring and fall have cooler temperatures, and late summer and early fall bring afternoon thunderstorms. Trail is fully exposed and there's no water after the visitor center, so be sure to have plenty of water, sunscreen, and a hat and consider earlier morning hikes on warm days.

**GET THERE** From Moab, take US-191 north for 11 miles. Turn left onto UT-313W and drive 14.6 miles. Continue onto Island in the Sky Road and drive for 19 miles until you reach the parking lot at the very end.

Google Maps: bit.ly/timbergrandview

**RESTROOMS** Yes

**FEE** $30 or Annual Pass

**TREAT YOURSELF** Moab Diner back in town is an old-fashioned treat, with a banana split that's perfect for cooling off after a trip to the viewpoint.

Canyonlands National Park
(435) 719-2313
Facebook @CanyonlandsNPS

an island in the sky, as the national park calls it. Squeeze through two huge boulders and find yourself at the point itself, the southernmost spot on the Island in the Sky. To your left, you'll see the Colorado River and the Needles District of Canyonlands. To your right is the Green River and the Maze District. Both rivers run together to make a confluence into the Colorado River and carved all the awesome canyons around you. Maybe one day you'll explore this backcountry! You can take in the view there at the edge, or, for older adventurers, it's an easy boulder up to the top of the rock at the end to get the grandest of views. Head back the way you came and consider camping at nearby Willow Flat Campground (no water) or at Dead Horse Point State Park (water available). Don't forget to grab your stamp and Junior Ranger badge at the visitor center!

# SCAVENGER HUNT

### Spire

The rocks below you are all made up of different compositions, some harder than others. Spires form when caps of harder rock protect the rock below them, making vertical towers like this one. Draw the spire in your nature journal, and think of other shapes and sizes spires can be.

How did this tower last when other parts eroded around it?

### Holes in the rock

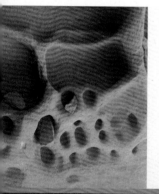

As you're walking on the mesa-top sandstone, look for these fun holes pocking the side of some of the rocks. What force of erosion do you think created these holes? Take small pebbles on the ground and create a pattern in the holes. Just be sure to leave no trace, and put them back down when you're done.

Holes created by erosion

### Plateau lizard

Can you spot this reptile? It's difficult because the lizard's coloring camouflages it in the desert so it can't be seen by predators like birds. Hang a sock  from the back belt loop of your pants and play lizard tag. Lizard tails can break off and regenerate if they're caught by predators, so if your hiking buddy pulls your "tail" off, you're still not out!

*Sceloporus tristichus* (*scleporus* means "leg holes" in Greek—notice the large pores in its legs)

### White Rim Road

Look down. Fourteen hundred feet below you lies a white crusty layer with a road heading across it. Do you see any Jeeps or off-road vehicles charging away? White Rim Road is a popular road for that kind of adventure. Would you ever take a car down there?

This layer of rock is a sandstone bench that caps the rock below it.

### Narrowleaf yucca

Look for long, narrow, pokey leaves on this plant. If you're visiting in spring, you might see a single 5-foot-tall flower stalk emerging from its center. Is it taller than you? The roots of narrowleaf yucca can be used to make soap. Do you think it smells like your soap at home?

*Yucca angustissima*

# 16

# GO BACK IN TIME AT HOVENWEEP RUINS

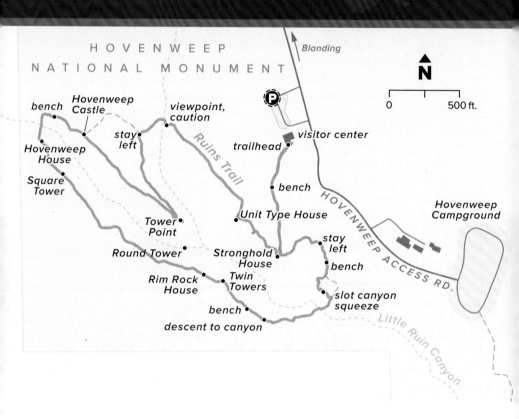

HOVENWEEP
NATIONAL MONUMENT

Blanding

N

0          500 ft.

bench
Hovenweep
Castle
viewpoint,
caution

stay
left

Ruins Trail

trailhead

visitor center

Hovenweep
House

Square
Tower

bench

Unit Type House

Hovenweep
Campground

Tower
Point

Round Tower

Stronghold
House

stay
left

bench

HOVENWEEP ACCESS RD.

Rim Rock
House

Twin
Towers

bench

descent to canyon

slot canyon
squeeze

Little Ruin Canyon

## YOUR ADVENTURE

Adventurers, today you're on the historical homelands of the Ancestral
Puebloans on the Cajon Mesa, a 500-square-mile raised block. Explore the
history of a civilization dating to the late 1100s, when communities began
to form around water sources. At the visitor center, start on a paved path.
You'll pass a bench, then the first junction at the Stronghold House. Turn

The Puebloan ruins at Hovenweep are more than 1000 years old →

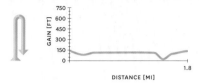

**LENGTH** 1.8 miles out and back

**ELEVATION GAIN** 141 ft.

**HIKE + EXPLORE** 1.5 hours

**DIFFICULTY** Easy—fairly level loop except for the final descent into the canyon on the way out

**SEASON** Year-round. Spring offers wildflower blooms and cooler temperatures, as does fall. In late spring and early summer you might find biting gnats, so bring long layers. Summer brings monsoons, possible flash floods, and hot temperatures, so consider visiting in the early morning and bring plenty of water and sun protection. Winter can bring snow and ice and the visitor center may close, so check the website or call for conditions.

**GET THERE** From Blanding, take US-191 south for 14.8 miles, and then turn left onto UT-262E and drive for 8.4 miles. Turn left onto Hovenweep Road and go 6.7 miles, then right on Reservation Road and drive 9.4 miles, then turn left on Hovenweep Road/Reservation Road and go 5 miles. Turn right at the sign on CR 268A, and the parking lot is straight ahead.

Google Maps: bit.ly/timberhovenweep

**RESTROOMS** Yes

**FEE** None

**TREAT YOURSELF** Relax after your hike at the old-school Patio Diner back in Blanding for great burgers and thick shakes.

Hovenweep National Monument
(970) 562-4282
Facebook @HovenweepNPS

right to take a counterclockwise loop along the edge of the ravine, with the Boulder House and Unit Type House. Continue to a viewpoint—be careful here. Stay left and make your way to Tower Point. Continue straight to the Hovenweep Castle, and turn left when you reach the main trail again. You'll see the Square Tower in the canyon and you'll curve around, passing Hovenweep House, Round Tower, Rim Rock House, and the Twin Towers. You'll then see the trail going down into the canyon. Carefully climb down, cross the bottom of the canyon, and then head back up. Stay left, passing a trail on your right to the campground. Turn right back toward the visitor center when you reach the Stronghold House. Consider staying at Hovenweep Campground, sleeping just where others have in the distant past.

# SCAVENGER HUNT

## Southwestern barrel cactus

Look at the fish-hooked shaped spines on this round succulent (a plant that holds water in its flesh). In the summer, yellow or red flowers sprout at the tops of barrel cactuses. The cactuses tend to lean toward the sun. Is the one you see leaning today?

*Ferocactus wislizeni* (*fero* is Latin for "ferocious")

## Unit Type House

Look closely here for living and storage rooms and a kiva—a room for rituals and political meetings. Most larger pueblos expanded by simply repeating this arrangement of rooms. Draw a floor plan of where you live now. How is it the same or different than this pueblo?

Unit Type House is the name archaeologists gave to a basic building plan at sites in the Southwest

### Hovenweep Castle

The farmers who lived in this canyon may have used this large structure as a dwelling, a community center, or a spiritual center. Look closely at the two D-shaped towers and their sandstone block walls. How are the stones stuck together? A wooden beam in one tower dates the structure to 1277—one of the latest dates of any structure in this region. Sketch in your nature journal what kind of sandstone structure you would construct if you lived here.

The largest of the preserved structures

### Square Tower

Hovenweep means "deserted valley" in the Ute and Paiute languages. Photographer William Henry Jackson adopted this name when he came upon the ruins in 1874 and documented the structures. Archaeologists use clues to build the story of the past. Based on the clues that you see, what do you think this tower was used for?

This tower is a perfect square; all sides are the same length

### Twin Towers

The Twin Towers had sixteen rooms. Can you make out how the two buildings rise from the bedrock, their walls almost touching? One tower is oval, and the other is horseshoe-shaped. Find a rock on the ground, and imagine how long it would take to build a tower from the rocks around you.

The two towers were built less than a foot apart but are not connected

# 17

# FIND THE ANCESTRAL PUEBLOAN RUINS IN BUTLER WASH

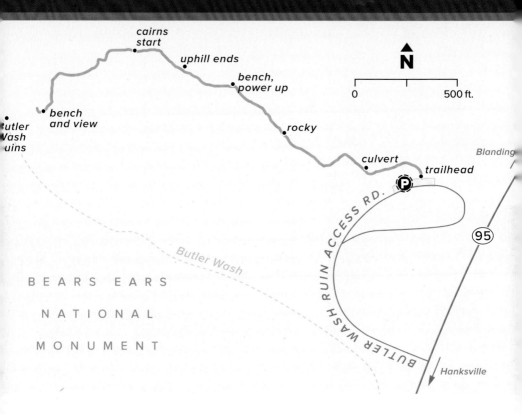

## YOUR ADVENTURE

Adventurers, today you're on the historical homelands of the Ancestral Puebloans. Between the years of approximately 500 and 1300, the caves and mesa tops surrounding Butler Wash were inhabited by the Puebloans. Members of the Basketmaker culture lived primarily on the mesa tops, using the caves for temporary shelter or burial areas. The site was

Butler Wash has an ancient city in the rocks →

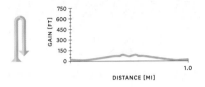

**LENGTH** 1.0 mile out and back

**ELEVATION GAIN** 108 ft.

**HIKE + EXPLORE** 1 hour

**DIFFICULTY** Easy—short, with a couple of areas of slickrock

**SEASON** Year-round. Trail is exposed to the sun, so remember water and sunscreen and consider going in the morning or early evening hours.

**GET THERE** From Blanding, take US-191 south for 4 miles. Turn right on UT-95N and drive 10.4 miles until the pullout for the trailhead on the right.

Google Maps: bit.ly/timberbutler

**RESTROOMS** Yes

**FEE** None

**TREAT YOURSELF** Grayson Ice Cream Parlor is back in Blanding. Grab homemade fudge or hand-dipped ice cream after touring the ruins.

Bears Ears National Monument
(435) 587-1500
Facebook @BLMUtah

abandoned around 1300 because of erosion, drought, depletion of natural resources, or pressure from tribes north of here. Are you ready to go back in time and see a city in the rocks? Sign the register at the trailhead, and let's go! The trail stays fairly flat for a while, but you'll soon begin to walk directly on the slickrock. Power up at one of the two benches along the trail. When the trail turns to rock, watch for cairns (small rock piles) to make your way. Once you do, you'll see the final bench overlooking the Puebloan ruins. Turn back the way you came and consider camping nearby at the Comb Wash Campground.

# SCAVENGER HUNT

### Ancient city

How many buildings can you count? Three round kivas and one square kiva—a structure built for ceremonial use—are located at the largest site. A total of twenty rooms, or structures, are located here, with several other storage rooms or granaries in small niches or protective alcoves around the canyon. Sketch them in your nature journal and label what you think the different areas might have been.

Ancestral Puebloan ruins at Butler Wash

### Fourwing saltbush

Look for these bright yellow flowers in the summer and fall. Archaeological research shows that the Ancestral Puebloans used fourwing saltbush to flavor pit-roasted corn. What sorts of plants do you use to flavor your food?

*Atriplex canescens*

### Fremont cottonwood

This water-loving deciduous tree that grows down at the bottom of the canyon loses its leaves in the fall. The Ancestral Puebloans used the tree's soft wood for roof beams and weaving tools. Have you ever cut wood before? If so, what did you use it for?

*Populus fremontii*

### Indian paintbrush

Look for the bright red of this plant in the summer and early fall. The color attracts pollinators like bees and hummingbirds. Actually, the red part isn't the flower. Those are technically bracts (a type of leaf) that protect the flower inside. Look closely. Can you spot it in there?

*Castilleja* sp.

### Mormon tea

Early Mormon pioneers used this plant for making tea, and American Indians have used it to treat ailments including colds, stomachaches, and skin sores. Look closely at the plant's skinny, jointed branches. How many joints can you find in just one branch?

*Ephedra viridis*

# 18

# LADDER-CLIMB DOWN TO SIPAPU NATURAL BRIDGE

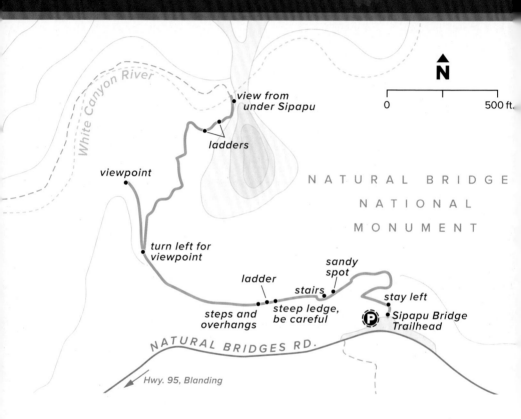

Map labels:
White Canyon River
view from under Sipapu
ladders
viewpoint
N
0   500 ft.
NATURAL BRIDGE NATIONAL MONUMENT
turn left for viewpoint
sandy spot
ladder
stairs
stay left
steep ledge, be careful
Sipapu Bridge Trailhead
steps and overhangs
NATURAL BRIDGES RD.
Hwy. 95, Blanding

## YOUR ADVENTURE

Adventurers, today you're on the historical homelands of the Ancestral Puebloans that sit atop Cedar Mesa. This landscape is made of whiter stone than the red sandstone you've seen in other parts of southern Utah. Over 260 million years ago, the area of Natural Bridges was actually a beach of dazzling white sand on the shoreline of the sea covering eastern Utah.

Imagine the force needed for water to carve out Sipapu Natural Bridge! →

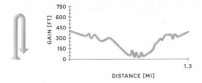

**LENGTH** 1.3 miles out and back

**ELEVATION GAIN** 404 ft.

**HIKE + EXPLORE** 2 hours

**DIFFICULTY** Challenging—involves three ladders and a steep descent into the bottom of the canyon

**SEASON** Year-round. Some areas are very exposed, so bring plenty of water and sunscreen. The park can get snow and ice and the entrance road can be closed after winter storms, so be sure to check ahead. Spring has wildflower blooms and cooler temperatures, as does fall. Late spring has biting gnats, so be sure to wear long sleeves.

**GET THERE** From Blanding, take US-191 south for 4 miles. Turn right on UT-95N and drive for 30.2 miles, turn right onto UT-275N and drive 4.4 miles, then turn right on Bridge View Drive to the entrance station. After the entrance station, drive another 2.7 miles and the parking will be on your right. This is a one-way loop, so you will need to travel 9 miles all the way around to leave the park.

Google Maps: bit.ly/timbersipapu

**RESTROOMS** Yes

**FEE** $20 or free with annual pass

**TREAT YOURSELF** Destination Awake in Blanding has coffee for lead adventurers and yummy baked goods to go to enjoy on the trail.

Natural Bridges National Monument
(435) 692-1234
Facebook @NaturalBridgesNPS

Over time, water spread and receded, depositing layers of sand, silt, and mud. The ancient sea's waves washed nearly all the darker minerals away here, leaving only white quartz sands behind. You'll begin on white rock and follow the cairns (small rock piles) as you zig and zag down. Soon you'll reach one set of stairs, then another. When you reach the sign, go left briefly to get a great view of Sipapu Bridge. Be careful on the ledge! You'll head back to the junction and down, climbing three ladders and using several sets of handrails until you're at the bottom of the bridge along White Canyon. Power up and then head back the way you came. Consider extending the adventure at Natural Bridges Campground by the visitor center.

# SCAVENGER HUNT

### Gambel oak

Look for this low-lying deciduous (loses its leaves) shrub's lobed leaves in the grove underneath Sipapu Bridge. Its brown acorns fall to the ground in autumn. If you find one, separate its cap from the body, stick the cap on your finger, and have a finger puppet show with your hike-mates!

*Quercus gambelii*

### Sipapu Bridge

This wonder is the second-largest natural bridge in the world! What's the difference between an arch and a bridge, you may ask? An arch is eroded by freezing and thawing and collected moisture from rainfall. Natural bridges like Sipapu are created when a river eventually breaks through the rock that was here. Then it's game over—a small hole can turn into a huge natural bridge like this from the force of the flow!

The view from under Sipapu Bridge

### Turkey vultures

These birds of prey fly around looking for carrion, or dead animals, on the ground. Their featherless heads help them eat without picking up germs. Look for their slow circling, swooping pattern in the sky and imitate it yourself by unfurling your own wings and swooping left to right above some dinner!

*Cathartes aura*

### Ladders

*Sipapu* is a Hopi word meaning "the place of emergence," representing a gate to the spirit world. The staff of the national monument have installed a series of three metal ladders to help you descend into and emerge again from the canyon. Can you count how many rungs are on each? Theodore Roosevelt recognized how special the landscape was here and declared this Utah's first national park unit in 1908.

The ladders require careful stepping

### Desert varnish

Can you spot the dark stripes running down the sides of the sandstone? These stains are made when a rainstorm flows over a cliff face. The water

provides a microhabitat for airborne bacteria that stick like glue to the surface and then eat the minerals. Some of the petroglyphs in this area were made when American Indians chiseled away the dark stain to reveal the light-colored sandstone underneath.

Black stripes color the sandstone

# 19

# LOOP AROUND GOBLIN VALLEY

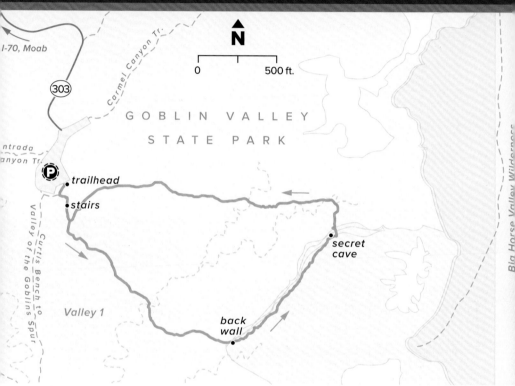

## YOUR ADVENTURE

Adventurers, today you're on the historical homelands of the Ute. Goblin Valley is at the southern end of the San Rafael Swell, a massive anticline (a fold of rock that shifts downward) that was uplifted 40 to 70 million years ago. From the parking lot, go down the stairs and generally head right to start your loop. Your goal is to head right, then turn left toward the back

Ready to explore this field of hoodoos? →

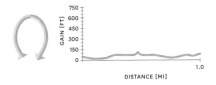

**LENGTH** 1.0-mile loop

**ELEVATION GAIN** 69 ft.

**HIKE + EXPLORE** 1 hour

**DIFFICULTY** Easy—a flat jaunt where you can always see the parking lot and not get lost; you can go further, however, so just make sure to keep the parking lot in sight

**SEASON** Year-round. Spring and fall are the best seasons, with days that are sunny and warm but not too hot. Summer gets extremely hot, so consider very early morning if you go during this time. Winter is snowy, but its adds a neat effect to the landscape. Trail can get muddy after rain or snow.

**GET THERE** From Hanksville, take UT-24 20 miles north. Turn left on Mount Temple Road and drive 5.2 miles, then left onto Goblin Valley road and go 6.9 miles. Stay left at the final junction and take it to the end of the road, which ends in a parking lot.

Google Maps: bit.ly/timbergoblin

**RESTROOMS** Yes

**FEE** $20; weekends in April, May, September, October $25

**TREAT YOURSELF** Stan's Burger Shak back down in Hanksville has yummy burgers and thick, tasty shakes that are perfect for a post-goblin power-up.

Goblin Valley State Park
(435) 275-4584
Facebook @GoblinValleyStatePark

canyon wall, then walk along the back canyon wall to look for a secret cave. Then you'll turn left to head back to the parking lot. When you're done, consider camping just down the road at Goblin Valley Campground and get the joy of watching these otherworldly structures in the sunset; you'll also experience one of Utah's best displays of stars—it's a Verified Dark Sky Park.

# SCAVENGER HUNT

### Hoodoo goblins

These hoodoos formed via gradual erosion of sandstone deposited 170 million years ago when this area was an ancient sea. Cracks developed in the rock, and softer layers eroded away. Wind and rain shaped the goblins into their eerie forms in a process called spheroidal weathering. This area used to be called Mushroom Valley. Draw your own goblins in your nature journal.

Twin hoodoos

### Russian thistle tumbleweed

You may see a mature one of these rolling along the road or on the trail today, doing what it does best—dispersing seeds, with more than 250,000 per ball. Can you tumble? Try your best to roll like a tumbleweed. Be sure to brush yourself off afterward!

*Salsola tragus*

### Secret cave

This cave is formed in the side of the cliff wall that surrounds and protects the goblin hoodoos. What do you think is inside? Be sure not to climb the hoodoos—they are fragile, and we want to leave them for others to explore.

A cave in the cliff face

### Saltlover

There are not many plants in Goblin Valley State Park, but this succulent (plant with fleshy leaves that hold water) loves the salt in the soil here. Saltlover sprouts many branches from the base and is absolutely covered with dense white and pink flowers in the summer. Take a whiff. What does it smell like?

*Halogeton glomeratus* (*hal* means "salt" in Greek)

### Caps of the Curtis Formation

Look for the geologically younger, grayish green Curtis Formation sandstone capping some of the rocks around you. These are remnants of marine reefs from the ancient seabed! The caps protect the softer rock below. Can you think of anything else hard that protects something softer below it?

Curtis Formation

# 20

# RUN UNDER HICKMAN NATURAL BRIDGE

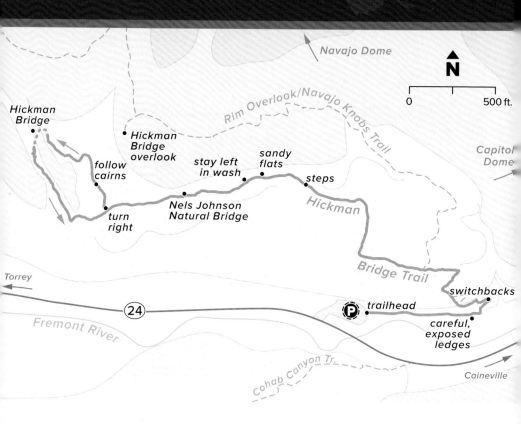

Hickman Bridge

Navajo Dome

**N**

0          500 ft.

Rim Overlook/Navajo Knobs Trail

Capitol Dome

Hickman Bridge overlook

follow cairns

stay left in wash

sandy flats

steps

Hickman

turn right

Nels Johnson Natural Bridge

Bridge Trail

switchbacks

Torrey

24

trailhead

Fremont River

careful, exposed ledges

Cohab Canyon Tr.

Caineville

# YOUR ADVENTURE

Adventurers, today you're on the historical homelands of the Fremont. We'll be hiking part of a nearly 100-mile-long warp in the Earth's crust called the Waterpocket Fold. Begin along the Fremont River, and soon you'll reach switchbacks leading you up. The trail flattens out a bit, then you'll reach another switchback. Keep heading up until you reach a sandy

Hickman Natural Bridge has a span of 133 feet →

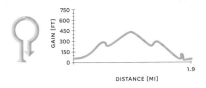

**LENGTH** 1.9-mile lollipop loop

**ELEVATION GAIN** 449 ft.

**HIKE + EXPLORE** 2 hours

**DIFFICULTY** Moderate—fairly short and wide trail, but a pretty steady uphill grind

**SEASON** Year-round. Trail is exposed, so be sure to bring plenty of water and sunscreen and avoid the heat of midday. Spring and fall offer cooler temperatures and avoiding the heat and monsoon rains of summer and the chance of snow in winter.

**GET THERE** From Torrey, head east on UT-24 for 12.6 miles until you reach the Hickman Bridge pullout.

Google Maps: bit.ly/timberhickman

**RESTROOMS** Yes

**FEE** $35 or free with annual pass

**TREAT YOURSELF** Just 3 miles west in Fruita is the Gifford Homestead, with fresh pies, cookies, and more in a historic building.

Capitol Reef National Park
(435) 425-3791
Facebook @CapitolReefNPS

wash—stay left here. On the right, look for the Nels Johnson Natural Bridge, a mini-bridge named after a homesteader who settled here in the early 1900s. Power up here. Soon you'll reach a fork—turn right to take the loop counterclockwise. Follow the cairns (small rock piles) to find the majestic Hickman Natural Bridge. Walk underneath it and then wind your way back to the fork to close the loop. Head back the way you came. When you're done, consider staying at the beautiful Fruita Campground just down the road.

# SCAVENGER HUNT

### Rabbitbrush

Check out these bright yellow flowers in the late summer and fall. American Indians have used rabbitbrush to make yellow dye, tea, and cough syrup. Be sure to watch what wildlife comes near it for at least 5 minutes. You'll likely spy a butterfly or other pollinator noshing on the plant's tubular flower clusters.

*Chrysothamnus* sp. ("golden shrub" in Latin)

### Hickman Natural Bridge

This natural wonder of Kayenta Formation sandstone was named after Joseph Hickman, who was a local school administrator and state legislator. He was an early conservation advocate for this area, which he called "Wayne Wonderland" (for Wayne County). What do you see here that you might like named after you?

View from under Hickman Natural Bridge

### Desert spiny lizard

This reptile is an ectotherm, a cold-blooded animal that obtains warmth from the environment by sunning on rocks. They become inactive during cold winter months. Desert spiny lizards have distinctive black marks on each side of their necks. They snack on insects, other lizards, and plant material. Find a warm rock and bask on it, pretending you aren't a warm-blooded mammal.

*Sceloporus magister*

### Black boulder

Look for these andesite lava rocks plopped around the area. Can you see the holes in the rock where gas was released as the rock cooled? These boulders were transported here—and rounded in the process—by large debris from melting glacier flows running off the volcanic peaks around you.

Igneous rock formed from lava

### Capitol Dome

Does this look like the Capitol Building in Washington, D.C., to you? This rock formation explains one part of the park's name—Capitol—but the other part comes from the rocks that look like barrier coral reefs in the ocean. Can you see those too?

This rounded rock structure looms over you on the trail

# 21

# SOAK IN THE VIEW AT SUNSET POINT

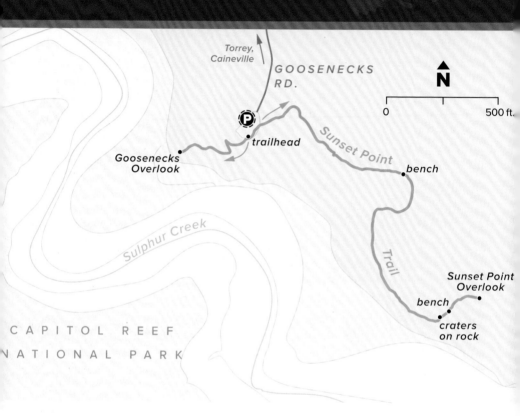

Torrey, Caineville

GOOSENECKS RD.

N

0    500 ft.

trailhead

Sunset Point

Goosenecks Overlook

bench

Sulphur Creek

Trail

Sunset Point Overlook

bench

craters on rock

CAPITOL REEF

NATIONAL PARK

# YOUR ADVENTURE

Adventurers, today you're on the historical homelands of the Southern Paiute. We'll explore this red rock paradise by first going to the right to check out Goosenecks Overlook, which is 500 feet down in a canyon. You'll be gazing out over the 5.8-mile-long Sulphur Creek that's carved

Sunset Point offers views of stunning red rock formations →

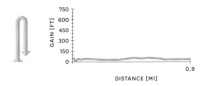

**LENGTH** 0.9 miles out and back (T-shaped)

**ELEVATION GAIN** 33 ft.

**HIKE + EXPLORE** 45 minutes

**DIFFICULTY** Easy—flat and short; just watch littles around the edges

**SEASON** Year-round. Trail is exposed, so be sure to bring plenty of water and sunscreen and avoid the heat of midday. Spring and fall offer cooler temperatures and avoiding the heat and monsoon rains of summer and the chance of snow in winter.

**GET THERE** From Torrey, take UT-24 for 8.3 miles and turn right onto Goosenecks Road. You'll first see Panorama Point; keep going on Goosenecks Road for 0.8 mile until it ends in the Sunset Point Parking Area.

Google Maps: bit.ly/timbersunsetpoint

**RESTROOMS** Yes

**FEE** $35 or free with annual pass

**TREAT YOURSELF** Slacker's Burger Joint in Torrey has great burgers, fries, and shakes.

Capitol Reef National Park
(435) 425-3791
Facebook @CapitolReefNPS

the landscape below you. Turn around to head back to the parking lot and take the next trailhead out to Sunset Point Overlook. Follow the skinny trail until you reach a bench. Power up here and continue on until you reach one more bench at the overlook and take in the view of Capitol Reef. How many different layers of rock can you see? Head back the way you came and consider staying the night at nearby Fruita Campground.

# SCAVENGER HUNT

### Layers

Look for these weird shapes on the rocks around you. The layers are the Moenkopi Formation and are 240 million years old. Can you see the ridges and benches carved out in them? Below it is the gray/yellow Kaibab Formation. Can you see the line between the two formations halfway through?

Layers on the rocks

### Colorado pinyon pine

You can identify the pinyon pine by its needles, which come bundled in groups of two, called fascicles. Be sure to look for a cone. The pine nuts hidden inside are eaten by many species of wildlife. In fact, the name *edulis* means "edible" in Latin. Can you make a pretend animal out of a cone? What creature does it look like to you?

*Pinus edulis*

## Utah juniper

Can you tell the difference between the pinyon pine and a juniper? Look at their needles. The pinyon pine's are smooth and pointy, but the juniper's are scales. If you find a juniper branch on the ground, dissect one of the needles to examine its scales. Rub it with your fingers, and then give them a good whiff.

*Juniperus osteosperma*

## Waterpocket Fold

The name Waterpocket Fold reflects this ongoing erosion of the rock layers. Water-pockets are small depressions that form in many of the sandstone layers as they are eroded by water. These are common throughout this geological wrinkle at Cap-itol Reef. Erosion of the tilted rock layers continues, forming colorful cliffs, massive domes, soaring spires, stark monoliths, twisting canyons, and graceful arches. How many of these features do you see today?

Part of the Waterpocket Fold

# 22

# WIND AROUND DEVIL'S GARDEN

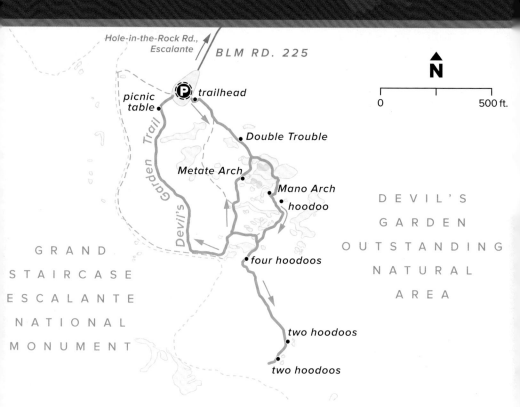

Hole-in-the-Rock Rd., Escalante

BLM RD. 225

N

0        500 ft.

picnic table

P trailhead

Double Trouble

Metate Arch

Mano Arch

hoodoo

Garden Trail

Devil's

four hoodoos

two hoodoos

two hoodoos

DEVIL'S GARDEN OUTSTANDING NATURAL AREA

GRAND STAIRCASE ESCALANTE NATIONAL MONUMENT

## YOUR ADVENTURE

Adventurers, today you're on the historical homelands of the Southern Paiute. You'll be exploring the eroded Entrada Sandstone of the great Grand Staircase steps around you. Even the road on which you come in is an adventure—it was made for the Hole-in-the-Rock Expedition of 1879. Sign the register before heading into the rock garden. From the parking lot, head

The Devil's Garden Trail winds through colorful hoodoos →

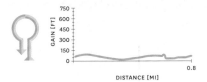

**LENGTH** 0.8-mile reverse lollipop

**ELEVATION GAIN** 92 ft.

**HIKE + EXPLORE** 1 hour

**DIFFICULTY** Easy—a short, flat, meandering loop

**SEASON** Year-round. Summer is extremely hot; go early in the morning and always bring plenty of water and sun protection. Spring and fall offer cooler temperatures, and winters can bring snow for a cool snowy landscape.

**GET THERE** From Escalante, take UT-12 5 miles east. Turn right on Hole-in-the-Rock Road and drive for 12.2 miles; the parking lot is on the right. The road is graded/gravel but can get treacherous after a rain. You can make the trip without a four-wheel-drive vehicle, but go slowly.

Google Maps: bit.ly/timberdevilsgarden

**RESTROOMS** Yes

**FEE** None

**TREAT YOURSELF** Escalante Outfitter's homemade pizza and pastries are a must post-adventure. You'll visit twice, it's so good.

Grand Staircase-Escalante National Monument (435) 644-1200
Facebook @BLMUtah

left to start this loop. First, you'll go by the Double Trouble feature. After a small mini-loop you'll come upon Mano Arch and a hoodoo, then curve around to close the mini-loop by going underneath Metate Arch. Head back toward the wash to see four more hoodoos, and finally end at a twin hoodoo. Stay left, on the outer edge of the loop, and end up at a picnic table and barbeque to power up after your exploration. Consider camping nearby at Calf Creek Campground to extend the adventure.

# SCAVENGER HUNT

### Grand Staircase

You are in the middle of the Grand Staircase of geological layers! The Grand Staircase is a geological wonder that climbs from the bottom of the Grand Canyon north, with the cliff edge of each rock layer forming giant steps. These steps are white, gray, pink, and

vermillion cliffs that rise 5500 feet from the base of the Grand Canyon to the Paunsaugunt Plateau in Bryce Canyon. How long do you think it took to create these different cliffs and terraces? Some of these cliffs are 275 million years old! When you get home, use watercolors or crayons to try to capture all the different colors you see.

Layers of the Grand Staircase

## Hoodoos

Entrada Sandstone has several layers. The bottom layer of the hoodoos on this trail is called Gunsight Butte Member, the middle is Cannonville Member, and the top is the smooth white Escalante Member. What do the hoodoos look like to you? Draw a hoodoo and label the layers you see.

A slew of hoodoos

## Metate and Mano Arches

Metate Arch is the more slender, and Mano Arch is the thicker one. A metate is a curved flat stone, like a mortar, and a mano is a tool similar to a pestle, used for grinding grains. Do you see why these formations might have been named after these tools?

Metate and Mano Arches

## Hole-in-the-Rock Road

On the very road you were on today, a train of eighty wagons holding 250 men, women, and children made their way here in December 1879. They were prepared with supplies for a six-week journey to establish a new community in southeastern Utah. Unfortunately the trek actually took them six months to complete. Could you have done that?

This painting by Glen S. Hopkinson shows a wagon train squeezing through Hole-in-the-Rock to create a shortcut.

# 23

# COOL OFF BY LOWER CALF CREEK FALLS

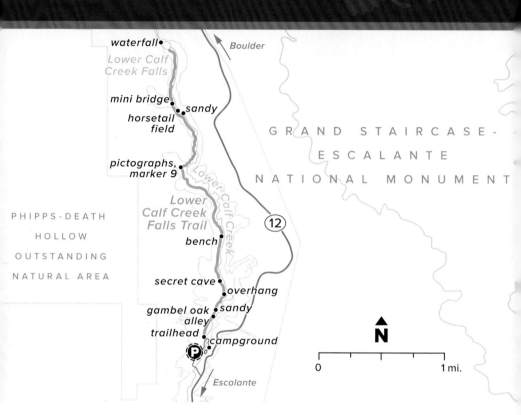

# YOUR ADVENTURE

Adventurers, today you're on the historical homelands of the Fremont, traveling through a box canyon—with a flat bottom and vertical walls, like a big box. You'll follow Lower Calf Creek all the way to the waterfall, passing by where pioneers once raised calves. Notice the lush cottonwoods all around the water. After the trailhead, you'll start to move away from the creek as

Take in the coolness of this 130-foot-high waterfall →

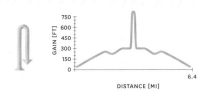

**LENGTH** 6.4 miles out and back

**ELEVATION GAIN** 820 ft.

**HIKE + EXPLORE** 3 hours

**DIFFICULTY** Challenging—our longest hike, with some sandy parts and some uphill; be sure to spend plenty of time powering up at the waterfall

**SEASON** Year-round. Spring and fall offer cooler temperatures, and the fall comes alive with the yellow cottonwoods. Can get warm in the summer—it's great for a summertime dip in the pool but hot on the trail—so try to go early or late in the day.

**GET THERE** From Escalante, take UT-12 15.7 miles, and turn left on the signed turn-out that goes down into the parking lot.

Google Maps: bit.ly/timberlowercalf

**RESTROOMS** Yes

**FEE** $5

**TREAT YOURSELF** Kiva Koffeehouse is just 2 miles north up UT-12. It has incredible views plus yummy fresh pastries and lunch items. Take them to go and snack at the falls!

Grand Staircase-Escalante National Monument
(435) 644-1200
Facebook @BLMUtah

you go through a Gambel oak alley, then pass an aspen grove on your right. You'll walk through a field of rabbitbrush, and then the sandy trail begins. After walking through this, you'll climb a few steps on red rock. Power up at the viewpoint and continue onward. Head under an overhang, pass a wide flat area, and check out a secret cave. After a bench, the trail starts to head up and get a bit rocky. You'll pass through another Gambel oak alley, then continue uphill. Be sure to stop at Trail Marker 9—look across the canyon for a pictograph of three large figures. You'll hit another sandy patch and walk through a horsetail field. Soon, though, you'll be cooling off in the creek and continuing along it until you reach a huge natural amphitheater and the waterfalls. Power up here and head back the way you came. Consider camping at the beautiful Calf Creek Campground for the weekend.

# SCAVENGER HUNT

### Fremont cottonwood

How thirsty are you today? These deciduous (loses their leaves) trees need a lot of water, so you'll find them growing by creeks and waterfalls. Collect as many of these triangular leaves as you can from the ground and make a mosaic out of them.

*Populus fremontii*

### Pictograph

Pictographs are images painted on rock, and petroglyphs are carved into a rock surface. The three large figures here were painted with red pigment sometime between 700 and 1300 by the Fremont people. Archaeologists think these figures could represent a significant event or a religious ceremony. What do you think this image represents?

Three large figures painted on the cliff face

### Boxelder

These deciduous trees also love water. Their roots help stabilize the ground at the bottom of the canyon. Look for their winged seeds, called samaras. If you find one, toss it and watch it spin it like a helicopter rotor.

*Acer negundo*

### Field horsetail

Horsetails are ancient plants that are related to the fern family, and they reproduce with spores, not seeds. Pioneers used these plants to scrub pots and pans, because the stems contain silica, which is gritty like sand. Do you help with the dishes at home? Would you be able to use these plants to clean?

*Equisetum arvense* (*equus* means "horse" in Latin)

### Desert globemallow

This wooly plant blooms with fun red balls during the summer and fall. The plant's multitude of flowers provides a steady source of pollen and nectar to honeybees and other insects. The plant has *globe* in its name because its seed is protected in a round sphere of petals. Look closely and try to find it!

*Sphaeralcea ambigua*

# 24

# COUNT THE SPIRES ON THE PANORAMA POINT

## YOUR ADVENTURE

Adventurers, today you're on the historical homelands of the Southern Paiute. You'll be exploring cool spires that formed from the middle Jurassic Period (180 million years ago) to the Cretaceous Period (95 million years ago). The park has nearly seventy of these tall rock towers, and you'll get up close and personal with a few on this trail. Begin on a flat trail through

You'll walk through a spire wonderland →

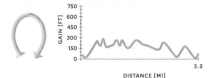

GAIN [FT]
750
600
450
300
150
0
3.2
DISTANCE [MI]

**LENGTH** 3.2-mile loop

**ELEVATION GAIN** 292 ft.

**HIKE + EXPLORE** 2.5 hours

**DIFFICULTY** Moderate—longer hike, but fairly flat terrain and not much uphill

**SEASON** Year-round. Late spring and fall are the most pleasant. Summer has thunderstorms and gets hot, so bring plenty of water and try to go early or late in the day. Winter can bring heavy snow.

**GET THERE** Take Kodachrome Road for 2.5 miles south of Cannonville and continue onto Cottonwood Canyon Road for 4.6 miles. Turn left onto Kodachrome State Park Road and drive for 1.5 miles. The parking will be on the right and the trailhead across the road.

Google Maps: bit.ly/timberpanorama

**RESTROOMS** Yes

**FEE** $10

**TREAT YOURSELF** Showdowns, 12 miles north in Tropic, has live music, a fun Western atmosphere, and burgers and fun desserts for the kids.

Kodachrome Basin State Park
(435) 679-8562
Facebook @KodachromeBasinStatePark

junipers to a fork—take this path counterclockwise. You'll begin an uphill and see a few spires on the right. Be sure to power up at Indian Cave and its bench. Keep going past another spire on your right, and soon you'll reach the Ballerina Spire. You'll soon come to the Hat Shop and then have a longer stretch to the turnoff to Secret Passage. Take this small loop clockwise and back on the main trail; keep going—you'll pass a side trail that goes to Cool Cave. Pass two spires on your left and then be sure to check out the Mammoth Spire Overlook. Continue straight and pass another trail going right that goes all the way up to Mammoth Spire. Take a final left to finish the loop. You can relax on this final stretch and then make your way back to the original fork. Stay straight here, and you'll find yourself back at the trailhead. When you're done, consider staying at one of three campgrounds in this International Dark Sky Park park: Basin, Bryce View, or Arch Campground.

# SCAVENGER HUNT

### Blue grama

These little plant caterpillars are so cute. But what exactly are they? It's a grass, and these curly parts are the seed head. Look closely and see if you can spot any dispersing in the wind! If you find one on the ground, make a grama-stache on your face.

*Bouteloua gracilis* ("slender" in Latin)

### Hat Shop

Kodachrome Basin was named in 1949 after the color film for the vivid changing colors you can see as the sun rises and sets in the park. How many colors do you see on the Hat Shop today? The spires are also called sedimentary pipes. Can you guess why?

How many different hats can you spot?

### Indian Cave

At the alcove called Indian Cave, there are thick marks in the rock that look like large handprints. Do you think people made the gouges? Or do you think it's a natural phenomenon? Do your hands fit into the etched fingers?

Odd marks on the rock face at Indian Cave

### Ballerina Spire

Geologists have a few theories about how these spires formed: The sand pipes may have been created by earthquakes that slowly shaped the forms or by ancient springs that cemented the sand together, or they may have formed underground from pressure in pockets of stone. How many different spires of Entrada Sandstone can you spot? Do you think this spire looks like a ballerina's foot? Tell your hiking buddy five other things it looks like to you.

A 30-foot tall sand pipe

### Roundleaf buffaloberry

Look for a silvery shrub with rounded leaves along the trail. It'll have yellow flowers in the spring and berries in the summer. Settlers thought the berries made a great sauce for buffalo meat. Feel its feathery soft leaves. What is one word that describes the way it feels to you?

*Shepherdia rotundifolia*

# 25

# HOODOO HUNT AT THE QUEENS GARDEN

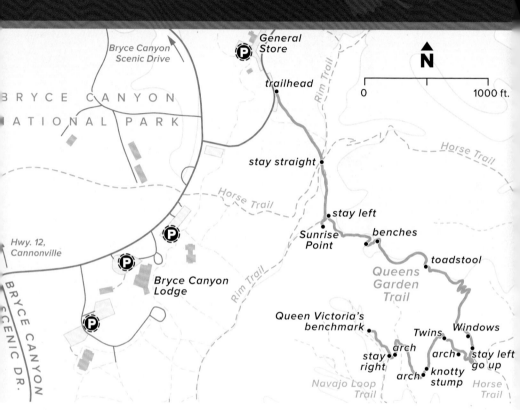

**Bryce Canyon Scenic Drive**

General Store

trailhead

Rim Trail

N

0          1000 ft.

B R Y C E   C A N Y O N
N A T I O N A L   P A R K

Horse Trail

stay straight

stay left

Horse Trail

Hwy. 12, Cannonville

Sunrise Point

benches

toadstool

Queens Garden Trail

Bryce Canyon Lodge

Rim Trail

Queen Victoria's benchmark

Twins   Windows

arch

stay right

arch

knotty stump

arch

stay left go up

Navajo Loop Trail

Horse Trail

B R Y C E   C A N Y O N
S C E N I C   D R.

## YOUR ADVENTURE

Adventurers, today you're on the historical homelands of the Southern Paiute to explore the largest concentration of hoodoos (irregular rock columns) in the world! Begin by heading to Sunrise Point to look out over the incredible valley before you and get the lay of the land. From here, head back to the trail and begin your journey down the switchbacks (take a power-up

It's time to find the Queens Garden! →

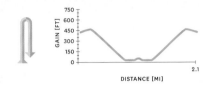

**LENGTH** 2.1 miles out and back

**ELEVATION GAIN** 453 ft.

**HIKE + EXPLORE** 2 hours

**DIFFICULTY** Moderate—a fairly level, wide trail; a fun downhill for the first half, and then you can take your time hiking up and back out

**SEASON** Year-round. Weather is highly variable in the fall, winter, and spring, including snow throughout. Summer offers comfortable temperatures.

**GET THERE** Take UT-63S 2.9 miles south of Bryce, and turn left onto Lodge Loop Road and go 0.5 mile. Turn left onto Sunrise Point Road, and find parking on the right.

Google Maps: bit.ly/timberqueens

**RESTROOMS** Yes

**FEE** $35 or free with annual pass

**TREAT YOURSELF** Make a night of it and bring the family to a live country show at Ebenezer's Barn and Grill just up the road in Bryce. They have a kid's barbeque menu.

Bryce Canyon National Park
(435) 834-5322
Facebook @BryceCanyonNPS
Instagram @BryceCanyonNPS_Gov

stop on the bench if you need it). Soon you'll pass some awesome toadstool formations and switchback down again. You'll hit a junction; stay right here and you'll soon go through an arch tunnel. Pass another bench, pass the Twins and a couple of more switchbacks, and go through another couple of arch tunnels to reach a junction. You'll go right here, to the Queens Garden. Head up just a little bit to get your amazing view! Power up and head back the way you came. Be sure to check out the visitor center to get your stamp and Junior Ranger badge. Consider extending the adventure by camping at Sunset or North Campground, right in the park.

# SCAVENGER HUNT

### Arch tunnel

Three small tunnels will help you make your way around the trail today. These pathways were blasted into the rock by workers using dynamite many years ago. What do you think it sounded like when it happened?

A man-made tunnel in the rock

### Toadstool hoodoo

How do you think the head of this formation has stayed on so long? Pick out another hoodoo and sketch it in your nature journal, adding details or setting it in a comic strip.

Do you think this hoodoo looks like a mushroom or something else?

### Ponderosa pine

These evergreen (keep their leaves) trees are some of the Southwest's largest trees. When they get older, these trees have orange, scaly bark that looks like dinosaur scales. Give the bark a sniff. Some people say it smells like vanilla or butterscotch!

*Pinus ponderosa* ("heavy pine" in Latin)

### Queen Victoria benchmark monument

Survey benchmark monuments are brass or metal disks in the ground that provide latitude, longitude, or height above/below sea level to help visitors understand the land. You made it! Now, take the Queen Victoria benchmark challenge: Lay a piece of paper from your nature journal over the circle and do a rubbing (or take a selfie with it), and bring it into the visitor center for a small reward!

This disk carries all the dignity of a royal seal

### More hoodoos

The formation of Bryce Canyon and its hoodoos required three steps: (1) deposition of rocks, (2) uplift of the land, and (3) weathering and erosion. When water freezes into ice, it expands by 9 percent! This causes tremendous pressure on the surrounding rock wherever water has trickled into crevices, and thus causes it to break apart. This process is known as ice wedging. Soft rock that started as a plateau eventually breaks down into walls, windows, and individual hoodoos.

Geological forces created these incredible sculptures

# 26

# BOUND AROUND THE BRISTLECONE PINE LOOP

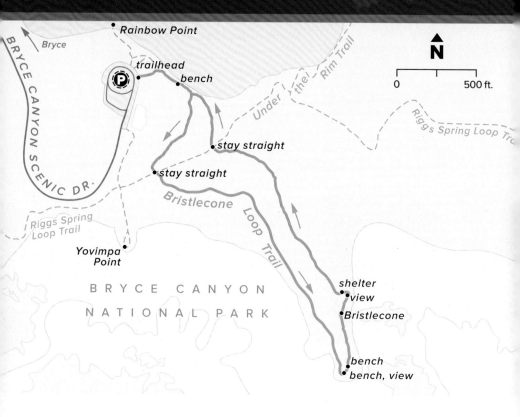

Rainbow Point

Bryce

trailhead

bench

P

BRYCE CANYON SCENIC DR.

Under the Rim Trail

N

0        500 ft.

Riggs Spring Loop Trl

stay straight

stay straight

Bristlecone Loop Trail

Riggs Spring
Loop Trail

Yovimpa
Point

B R Y C E   C A N Y O N

N A T I O N A L   P A R K

shelter

view

Bristlecone

bench

bench, view

## YOUR ADVENTURE

Adventurers, today you're on the historical homelands of the Southern Paiute on the Paunsaugunt Plateau. Take the trailhead right from the parking lot, and you'll take this loop clockwise. You'll have a view of Bryce Canyon (named after Mormon settler Ebenezer Bryce) on your left the whole time, but be sure to be looking in the air and in the pines for bird

Amazing viewpoints await at Rainbow Point! →

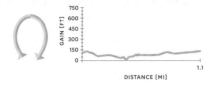

GAIN [FT]
750
600
450
300
150
0

1.1

DISTANCE [MI]

**LENGTH** 1.1-mile loop

**ELEVATION GAIN** 118 ft.

**HIKE + EXPLORE** 1 hour

**DIFFICULTY** Easy—fairly flat with a level surface but it's at an elevation of 9000 feet, so take it easy if you're feeling short of breath

**SEASON** Year-round. Weather is highly variable in the fall, winter, and spring, including snow throughout. Summer offers comfortable temperatures.

**GET THERE** Take UT-63S 19.3 miles south of Bryce until the road ends at the Rainbow Point parking lot.

Google Maps: bit.ly/timberbristlecone

**RESTROOMS** Yes

**FEE** $35 or free with annual pass

**TREAT YOURSELF** The Lodge at Bryce Canyon just up the road has a good kid's menu and a beautiful stone fireplace, a perfect spot for both young and older hikers to relax.

Bryce Canyon National Park
(435) 834-5322
Facebook @BryceCanyonNPS
Instagram @BryceCanyonNPS_Gov

life too. Soon you'll reach a shelter and a viewpoint—power up here. Head uphill a bit and pass a bristlecone pine on your left, then you'll reach a bench and another viewpoint. Be sure to check out the old bristlecone, and do a rubbing of the Bristlecone Loop benchmark with a piece of paper and pencil/pen—take it into the visitor center for a small reward! Close the loop by passing straight through a junction and find yourself back where you started. Be sure to check out the visitor center to get your stamp and Junior Ranger badge. Consider extending the adventure by camping at Sunset or North Campground, right in the park.

# SCAVENGER HUNT

### Steller's jay

Look for the awesome mohawk of this black and brilliant blue songbird. Like other jays, this bird is bold, curious, and very noisy. Steller's jays love snacking on all the pine trees in the area. Try to make your hair look like a Steller's jay's crest, then take a selfie!

*Cyanocitta stelleri*

### Douglas fir

People say that the three-pronged bracts on the scales of the Douglas fir's cone look like a little mouse tail. The cones of Douglas fir hang down from the branches, while other firs on this trail grow cones sticking straight up near the top. Try to crush one of the needles on the ground and see if you can smell its lemony scent.

*Pseudotsuga menziesii*

### Great Basin bristlecone pine

This tree might be up to 1800 years old! The oldest living bristlecone tree in the world is called Methuselah; it lives in California and is over 4790 years old! Look closely and count how many needles are grouped together in a bunch, called a fascicle. Bristlecones grow five needles together. What would you name this tree?

*Pinus longaeva* ("ancient" in Latin)

### Common raven

Look in the sky for the world's largest songbird! Ravens are very intelligent, and their squawks are like a language to other birds and animals. They even team up with each other to steal food from bear-proof garbage cans. Squawk and talk raven to your hiking buddy for the next 2 minutes. Can you communicate effectively?

*Corvus corax*

### Peregrine falcon

People have trained falcons for hunting for more than 1000 years, and the peregrine was always one of the most prized birds. These birds of prey usually fly at about 30 miles per hour, but they can dive at over 200 miles per hour! Do your best impression of a peregrine falcon in flight.

*Falco peregrinus* ("wandering" in Latin)

# 27

# WALK THE WASH TO RED HOLLOW SLOT CANYON

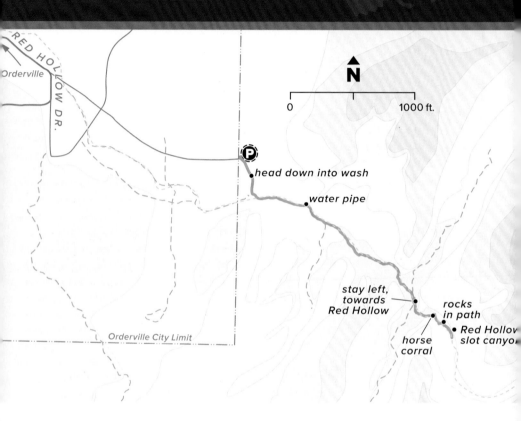

## YOUR ADVENTURE

Adventurers, today you're on the historical homelands of the Southern Paiute. From the parking lot, follow the trail as it leads down into a wash, a dry creek that temporarily fills with water when there is rain. There are multiple paths here—choose any, as they all lead down to the wide wash that leads you straight to the canyon. Here, bright red starts to appear on

Are you ready to feel the squeeze of the Red Hollow slot canyon? →

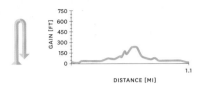

GAIN [FT]

750
600
450
300
150
0

1.1

DISTANCE [MI]

**LENGTH** 1.1 miles out and back

**ELEVATION GAIN** 207 ft.

**HIKE + EXPLORE** 1.5 hours

**DIFFICULTY** Moderate—it takes a bit to find the wash from the parking lot; the wash can be challenging as you walk in the sand exposed, and once in the slot canyon, you may need to negotiate narrow portions and cross over a couple of boulders

**SEASON** Year-round. Hot in the summer, so go early in the day and bring sun protection and plenty of water. Best in the spring and fall for moderate temperatures. Avoid days with thunderstorms or rain in the forecast, as the area is prone to flash floods.

**GET THERE** Take 100E in Orderville for 0.2 mile and then left onto Red Hollow Drive. Stay straight, as this turns to a good dirt road until it ends at a dirt parking lot.

Google Maps: bit.ly/timberredhollow

**RESTROOMS** No, but plenty down the road in Orderville

**FEE** None

**TREAT YOURSELF** The Rock Stop in Orderville sells rocks as well as frozen yogurt and mini-donuts.

BLM Kanab Field Office
(435) 644-1200
Facebook @BLMUtah

the wash bottom and its walls start to move in closer. You'll pass a small wash on the left—ignore this one and keep going straight—and likewise pass another small wash on the right. The slot canyon will be straight in front of you. Explore the narrow walls once inside, climbing over the few rocks in the path. You'll finally come to an end that's too high to safely climb. Turn back, soaking in the fun of the slot canyon before you do.

# SCAVENGER HUNT

### Red Hollow slot canyon

A slot canyon is a very narrow gorge with steep, high walls that are often made from soft rock such as sandstone. This area of Utah has more than 1000 of these special, narrow canyons. Flash floods, which happen when torrential rain causes powerful rushes of water, helped form the swirls and rounded forms you see as you walk through this canyon today. What's the narrowest this slot canyon gets?

Red Hollow slot canyon

### Ponderosa pine

These evergreen (keeps their leaves) trees have both male and female cones. The male ones are much smaller and release little pollen grains that float and sprinkle from tree to tree to fertilize the larger female cones. The sharp prickles at the ends of the female cone protect the growing seed inside from critters who might want to eat it. Once the seeds are mature, the cone's scales open and release them.

*Pinus ponderosa* ("heavy pine" in Latin)

### Prickly pear cactus

The red fruit of this succulent (plant with fleshy leaves that hold water) is known as a pear or tuna, and some people eat them—after removing the spines, of course. The green pads are also a vegetable, and people cook them as well. Which sounds more delicious to you?

*Opuntia* sp.

### Gambel oak

Traditionally, American Indians in the Southwest would grind the acorns of Gambel oak to make a kind of porridge. This deciduous tree loses its lobed leaves in the fall. If you find one on the ground, trace it in your nature journal. How many lobes does it have? How is it different from a pine needle? Why do you think that is?

*Quercus gambelii*

### Elkheart Cliffs

Along the trail, the deep red sandstone stops abruptly and is topped by a whiter material. Can you count how many red and white layers make up these dramatic cliffs? This is made up of Navajo Sandstone, a sedimentary rock.

The dramatic colors of Elkheart Cliffs

# 28

# CLIMB YOUR WAY INTO THE KANAB SAND CAVES

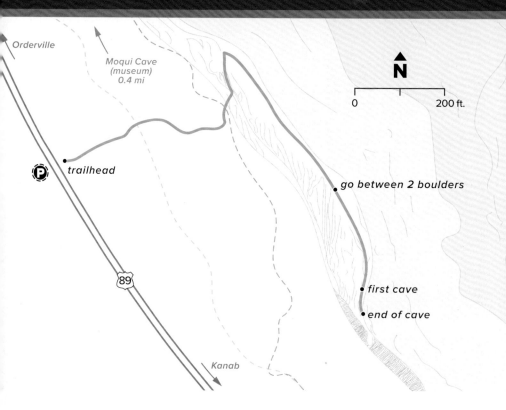

Orderville

Moqui Cave
(museum)
0.4 mi

N

0 — 200 ft.

P trailhead

go between 2 boulders

89

• first cave

• end of cave

Kanab

## YOUR ADVENTURE

Adventurers, today you're on the historical homelands of the Ute. Carefully cross the road and begin the hike by heading through the shrubs and walking to the base of the rock. From here, you'll walk sideways up to the left at an angle and then zigzag back to the right until you're on the fairly level ledge. You'll then walk to the right the whole way to the cave.

Which entry will you use at this Kanab Sand Cave? →

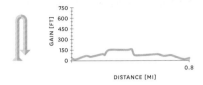

**LENGTH** 0.8 miles out and back

**ELEVATION GAIN** 157 ft.

**HIKE + EXPLORE** 1 hour

**DIFFICULTY** Challenging—there is a scramble to get up the rock, so best for older adventurers unafraid of heights; be sure to wear good shoes

**SEASON** Year-round. Summer is warm, so consider early morning and be sure to wear sun protection and bring plenty of water. Spring, winter, and fall offer much cooler temperatures.

**GET THERE** From Kanab, take US-89 north for 5.4 miles—there is a small unmarked parking lot on the left before you reach Moqui Cave. Once there, carefully cross the road and follow the well-worn path toward the caves that you can see ahead of you.

Google Maps: bit.ly/timbermoqui

**RESTROOMS** Yes, just up the road at Moqui Cave

**FEE** None

**TREAT YOURSELF** The Cave Cafe just up the road has smoothies and more to cool you off after your adventure.

BLM Kanab Field Office
(435) 644-1200
Facebook @BLMUtah

Be careful here as you walk toward the opening. Once you arrive, head inside on the soft sand. Look out the first entryway (being careful, as there is a sheer drop-off) and then explore the second and the third openings. When you reach the end of the cave, turn back the way you came. On the descent, follow the same slanted/zigzag path—it will always be easier than going straight down.

# SCAVENGER HUNT

### Caves

These man-made caves have sandy floors under smooth rock. They were excavated to harvest sand for glass production in the 1970s. To make sand melt, you need to heat it to roughly 3090°F, which is about the same temperature a space shuttle reaches as it reenters Earth's atmosphere. What would you like to make out of glass?

Kanab Sand Cave

### Fragrant sumac

Look closely at these hardy little shrubs on your approach to the rock. Fragrant sumac is known for being drought-tolerant. The shrubs produce bright red fruits in the summer, and their round-lobed leaves turn a bright orange in the fall. This plant is called *aromatica* for a reason—gently rub a leaf between your fingers and take a whiff. What do you smell?

*Rhus aromatica*

## Natural colors

Utah has many famous pictographs, images drawn by American Indians long ago. However, the colors and shapes in these rocks were made naturally. Do you see any shapes in them that remind you of other things? Draw them in your nature journal!

Red and yellow coloring on the rocks

## Sand sage

Look for these feathery shrubs as you approach the ascent. It loves the sand. Rub some of it on your wrist to apply "cowboy cologne." Do you like the way it smells? Tiny yellow flowers bloom in the spring and the fall. See if you can spot any today.

*Artemisia filifolia*

# 29

# DUNEWALK AROUND THE CORAL PINK SAND DUNES

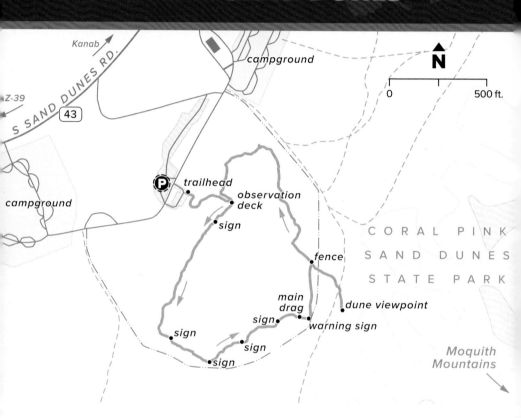

# YOUR ADVENTURE

Adventurers, today you're on the historical homelands of the Southern Paiute. The pink sand underneath you comes from the quartz in the Navajo Sandstone topping Moccasin Terrace. Look around—there's a perfect gap that allows sand to blow *in*, but the Moquith Mountains block the sand from blowing *out*, so it stays here. From the observation deck, start a clockwise

Coral Pink Sand Dunes are around 10,000–15,000 years old! →

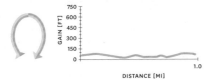

**LENGTH** 1.0-mile loop

**ELEVATION GAIN** 59 ft.

**HIKE + EXPLORE** 1.5 hours

**DIFFICULTY** Moderate—walking in sand can be a bit of a challenge

**SEASON** Year-round. Can get warm in the summer, so try to go early or late in the day. Best in spring for wildflowers and fall for cooler temperatures.

**GET THERE** Take US-89 for 7.4 miles north of Kanab. Turn left onto Hancock Road and drive for 9.4 miles. At the T intersection, turn left onto Coral Pink Sand Dunes Road/Highway 43 and drive for 3.2 miles, then turn left into the park. After the entrance gate, drive 0.1 mile and park in the parking lot on your left. You can also go all the way to the end to the campground to park, but you'll have to walk back.

Google Maps: bit.ly/timbercoraldunes

**RESTROOMS** Yes

**FEE** $10

**TREAT YOURSELF** Kanab Creek Bakery, 20 miles back in Kanab, has fresh baked goods and hot croque monsieurs.

Coral Pink Sand Dunes State Park
(435) 648-2800
Facebook @CoralPinkSandDunes

loop by heading right. Follow the nature trail signs to see if you can spot them all. Pass your first sign and continue straight, through the pink sand. You'll come upon another sign; head left here. You'll find three more signs before hitting the main drag, a wide sandy path that most people follow out to the main dune. You can head right here at the fence to go to the viewpoint of the large dune or continue farther on to climb the dune—and maybe even sand-sled down it by renting a sled or sandboard at the visitor center! Stay to the right to complete the sandy loop. Be sure to check out the visitor center and ask about their Junior Ranger badge. Consider camping out at the park campground just next to the trailhead.

# SCAVENGER HUNT

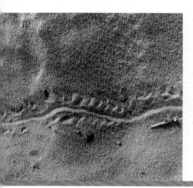

### Tracks

Your job today, adventurers, is to spot at least two different animal tracks. (Humans don't count!) This means you need to look closely, like a detective. Think about this one to start: What might leave a skinny line with a small mark to either side?

Animal tracks in the sand

### Badlands mule-ears

Pet these rough leaves shaped like mule's ears. Everything here is adapted to the desert—the fuzz helps with water loss by diffusing the sun's rays. Look for their bright yellow flowers in the summer. How does your body adapt to the heat?

*Scabrethia scabra* subsp. *attenuata*

### Nebkhas

Life is hard out here. Plants know it and adapt by growing in low mounds called nebkhas, or hummocks. As sand accumulates around where they're growing, they send out stems underground, called rhizomes, so they can sprout new plants a little ways away and start over. See if you can spot a connector stem sticking out between plants. Why do you think the plants don't grow on the very top of the dunes?

Look for these small lumps in the sand.

### Kanab yucca

Look for a tall bloom on this shrub in the spring and early summer. Only *one* insect can pollinate this plant, a yucca moth! Feel the plant's leaves; they probably seem waxy. Can you guess why this is a good feature to have when there's little water around?

*Yucca kanabensis* and its pollinator, *Tegeticula*

# 30

# TREK AROUND THE TOADSTOOLS

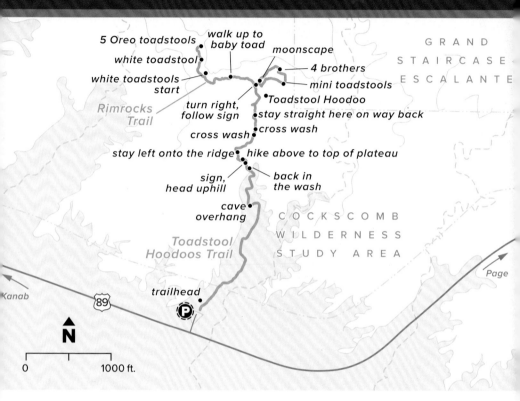

5 Oreo toadstools

walk up to baby toad

moonscape

white toadstool

4 brothers

white toadstools start

mini toadstools

Rimrocks Trail

turn right, follow sign

Toadstool Hoodoo

stay straight here on way back

cross wash

cross wash

stay left onto the ridge

hike above to top of plateau

sign, head uphill

back in the wash

cave overhang

GRAND STAIRCASE ESCALANTE

COCKSCOMB WILDERNESS STUDY AREA

Toadstool Hoodoos Trail

Page

trailhead

Kanab

89

N

0        1000 ft.

## YOUR ADVENTURE

Adventurers, today you're on the historical homelands of the Ancestral Pueblos in the Paria Rimrocks badlands, an eroding area on a step of the Grand Staircase. Begin this trek by walking toward the desert in a wash— an area that water flows down during storms. Pass a cool cave overhang, and then watch for the sign on the right that leads you uphill, where you'll

Toadstool Hoodoo greets you at the end of your hike →

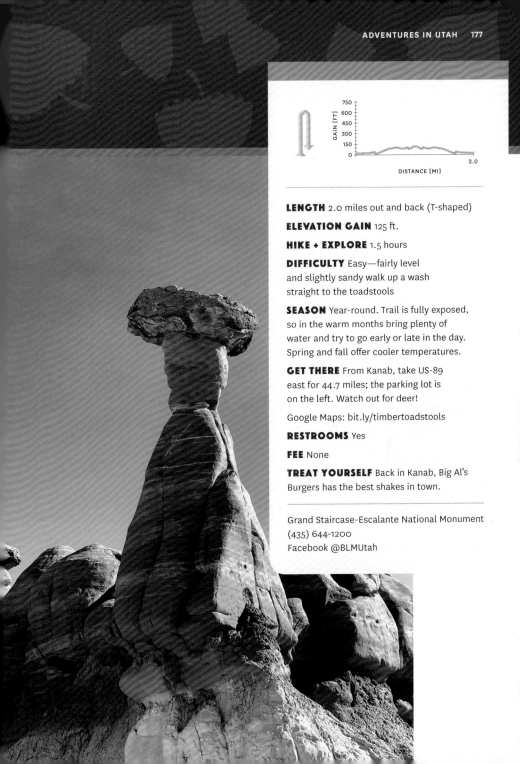

750
600
450
300
150
0

GAIN [FT]

2.0

DISTANCE [MI]

**LENGTH** 2.0 miles out and back (T-shaped)

**ELEVATION GAIN** 125 ft.

**HIKE + EXPLORE** 1.5 hours

**DIFFICULTY** Easy—fairly level and slightly sandy walk up a wash straight to the toadstools

**SEASON** Year-round. Trail is fully exposed, so in the warm months bring plenty of water and try to go early or late in the day. Spring and fall offer cooler temperatures.

**GET THERE** From Kanab, take US-89 east for 44.7 miles; the parking lot is on the left. Watch out for deer!

Google Maps: bit.ly/timbertoadstools

**RESTROOMS** Yes

**FEE** None

**TREAT YOURSELF** Back in Kanab, Big Al's Burgers has the best shakes in town.

Grand Staircase-Escalante National Monument
(435) 644-1200
Facebook @BLMUtah

climb to the top of a small red rock plateau. Stay left on the ridge, cross two more washes, and soon a Toadstool Hoodoo will come into view. Check it out from every side and then head to the right and explore some mini toadstools, the four brothers, and a few white toadstools. Continue back toward Toadstool Hoodoo and pass it to find even more toadstools. Eventually, you'll ascend slightly and head to the right to a little nook in the canyon hiding some special white toadstools with chocolate tops! Explore here, power up, and head back the way you came. Be sure to stay straight on your way back, ignoring side trails.

# SCAVENGER HUNT

### White toadstools

These white toadstools grow in their own little garden. How are they different from the red sandstone toadstools? Do the colors remind you of any of your favorite sweet treats?

White toadstools

### Sand sagebrush

Look for these bushes cropping up on the first part of the wash. Their silvery blue leaves grow in little bundles, and the yellow flowers appear in late summer. What features of this plant do you think might help it grow here, in hot and challenging conditions?

*Artemisia filifolia*

### Sego lily

If you're here in the spring, hopefully you'll be lucky enough to spot Utah's state flower! It grows 10 to 20 inches tall from a bulb in the ground. Look closely and count the three large white petals, the three white skinnier sepals (that protect the bud), and lilac or purple stripes in the middle. The Ute Indians taught Mormon settlers to eat the bulbs of this lily when food was scarce. What do you like to eat when you're really hungry?

*Calochortus nuttallii* (*calochortus* means "beautiful grass" in Greek)

### Toadstool Hoodoo

This toadstool formed when boulders of the roughly 100 million year old Dakota Formation fell downslope onto the softer Entrada Sandstone (formed around 160 million years ago), sheltering this softer rock from erosion. Play in the dirt—make a little spire and then put a small rock on top. Can you see how it could protect everything underneath from rain erosion?

Count the layers

# 31

# FOLLOW THE PATH TO CASCADE FALLS

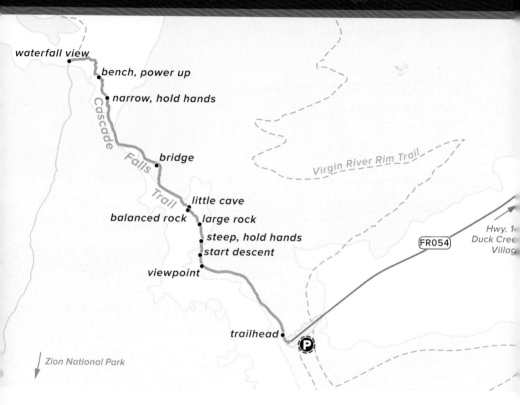

waterfall view

bench, power up

narrow, hold hands

Cascade Falls Trail

bridge

little cave

balanced rock

large rock

steep, hold hands

start descent

viewpoint

Virgin River Rim Trail

FR054

Hwy. 1
Duck Cree
Villag

trailhead

Zion National Park

## YOUR ADVENTURE

Adventurers, today you're on the historical homelands of the Southern Paiute in the 2 million acres of Dixie National Forest. Start at the trail sign at the northwest end of the parking lot and begin to gradually go up. You'll glimpse an expansive view of the north side of Zion National Park. At the designated viewpoint, make sure to stay behind the fence. Descending,

These cliffs provide a drop of 120 feet for Cascade Falls →

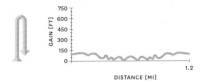

**LENGTH** 1.2 miles out and back

**ELEVATION GAIN** 125 ft.

**HIKE + EXPLORE** 1 hour

**DIFFICULTY** Moderate—starts easy and level, then descends along an exposed ledge, so keep littles close; climbs up gently to the waterfall lookout

**SEASON** Open spring, summer, and fall; road access closes in winter; call in October to see when it closes. Summer and fall can get hot, so try to go early or late in the day. Fall has beautiful foliage. Spring offers the best flow in the waterfalls.

**GET THERE** From Duck Creek Village, head 2 miles west on Highway 14 and turn left onto FR059. After 0.2 mile, make a slight right onto FR370. Drive for 1.5 miles and then turn left onto FR054. Drive 1.7 miles to the trailhead.

Google Maps: bit.ly/timbercascadefalls

**RESTROOMS** Yes

**FEE** None

**TREAT YOURSELF** Stop and get a slice of pie with ice cream from Aunt Sue's Chalet, about 6 miles east in Duck Creek Village.

Dixie National Forest
(435) 865-3700
Facebook @USFSDNF

cross a bridge to find yourself with a tall mountain to your right and an exposed cliff on your left—hold the hands of younger ones here. The trail is nice and wide, just be cautious. As you climb down, check out the fun little overhangs you can sit in and the small trickles of water coming right out of the mountain. The trail will start to climb back up and, before you know it, you'll be at the lookout standing right over Cascade Falls. Power up here and head back the way you came. Consider spending the weekend at nearby Duck Creek Campground.

# SCAVENGER HUNT

### Wyoming Indian paintbrush

The state flower of Wyoming, it's also found in many other states in the West, including Utah and Nevada. The upper red flower looks like a brush dipped in red paint, which is how it got its name. Look closely—the red structures aren't actually flower petals, but bracts, a type of leaf. Can you find the actual yellow tubular flower inside?

*Castilleja linariifolia*

### Ponderosa pine

These evergreen trees can grow to over 200 feet tall with a circumference of over 300 inches! Try to give the trunk a hug. How big is the circumference compared to your arms? They can live for 500 years or more. Large cracks in their often reddish trunks help you identify ponderosa pines. Smell the bark; some people say it smells like vanilla or butterscotch. Do you agree?

*Pinus ponderosa* ("heavy pine" in Latin)

### Balancing rock

Because of the steep incline and how fragile limestone can be, rocks often roll down the mountain. On this trail, you will come to a large rock that is perched precariously on another. How much longer do you think it will stay like that?

A teetering, tottering boulder

### Hoodoo formation

Watch for these rumpled-looking rock formations in the limestone. It takes millions of years for a hoodoo to form. There are different ways they can be created, but wind, ice, and rain are the main forces of erosion that create them. What do you think the formations will look like in a million years? Sketch a before and after of one in your nature journal.

The rocks around you are over 50 million years old

### Cascade Falls

Hop on the platform and take a look over the railing at the waterfall. The water from Cascade Falls comes from Navajo Lake, through an underground lava tube. After the falls, the water continues on to the Virgin River, through Zion, empties into Lake Mead, then joins the Colorado River. The waterfall is at its fullest in the spring due to mountain runoff and snowmelt. In late summer or early fall, you may only see a trickle. How far into the lava tube can you see?

This waterfall comes out of the side of the cliff

# 32

# SCRAMBLE YOUR WAY TO HIDDEN HAVEN FALLS

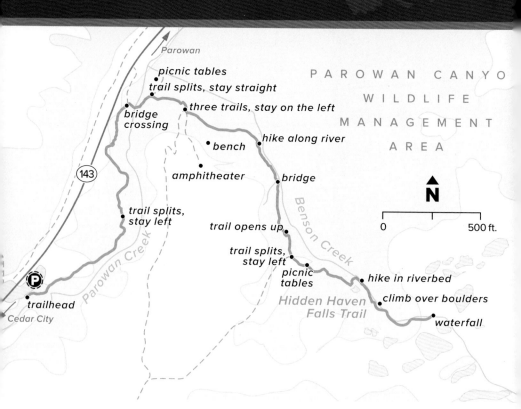

Map labels:

Parowan

picnic tables

trail splits, stay straight

three trails, stay on the left

PAROWAN CANYON WILDLIFE MANAGEMENT AREA

bridge crossing

bench

hike along river

143

amphitheater

bridge

Benson Creek

N

trail splits, stay left

trail opens up

0          500 ft.

Parowan Creek

trail splits, stay left

picnic tables

hike in riverbed

Hidden Haven Falls Trail

climb over boulders

trailhead
Cedar City

waterfall

## YOUR ADVENTURE

Adventurers, today you're on the historical homelands of the Southern
Paiute. This hike may result in some wet feet, so wear appropriate shoes!
You're exploring Parowan Canyon among rock layers that all come from
a volcanic eruption from the nearby Beaver Mountains. The trail starts
through a gap in a wooden fence—stay left at the first junction. You'll come

Twenty-foot Hidden Haven Falls is dramatic even when the flows are frozen →

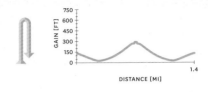

**LENGTH** 1.4 miles out and back

**ELEVATION GAIN** 275 ft.

**HIKE + EXPLORE** 1 hour

**DIFFICULTY** Challenging—easy trail but with some tricky spots to pass that will likely need an adult's help

**SEASON** Year-round. Spring, summer, and fall are the best times. Spring has the best waterfall flow, and fall has great foliage. In winter will need proper footwear (snowshoes or spikes) and might catch a frozen waterfall!

**GET THERE** From I-15N, take Exit 75 for UT-143 toward Parowan. After 0.4 mile, turn right onto UT-143. Drive 2 miles and then turn left onto S Main Street. Turn right onto Center Street. Drive for 6 miles and pull into the dirt parking lot on the left side of the road marked for Hidden Haven Falls.

Google Maps: bit.ly/timberhiddenhaven

**RESTROOMS** No

**FEE** None

**TREAT YOURSELF** Grab yourself a slice of homemade pie from Hamburger Patty's, 6 miles north in Parowan.

Utah Division of Wildlife Resources, Parowan Canyon Wildlife Management Area
(435) 865-6100
Facebook @UtahDWR

to a bridge across Parowan Creek. Pass two picnic tables, then continue up the trail and you'll come to a bench where there are three trails you can take. They are not marked, so be sure to follow the trail on the far left—it is the widest and stays relatively flat. You'll pass another bench on your right, then come to Benson Creek, which you can splash your feet in or continue on the trail that is just to the right of the creek. The trail gains a little in elevation and opens up to a beautiful view of mountains ahead. At the next split in the trail, stay on the left trail (unmarked). Remember that you are hiking to a waterfall, so you want to be sure to stay close to the creek. Pass another picnic bench, and when you come to a wide riverbed hop down inside and continue hiking upriver. Next are a couple of tricky spots where you'll need to climb over some rocks. Before you know it, you will be at Hidden Haven Falls! Power up and head back the way you came.

# SCAVENGER HUNT

### Wild licorice

This riparian plant grows along streams and rivers. It isn't used to make the candy, but its roots do have a licorice flavor. It was used as an herbal remedy to help cure fevers, stomachaches, and sore throats. Do you know any other plants used as a medicine?

*Glycyrrhiza lepidota* (derived from the Latin word for "scaled")

### Scarlet gilia

Look for these bright red splashes in the summer months. If you're lucky enough to spot one, get down low and look carefully into its tube. Can you see any nectar inside? See if you can trace one of the tubes or the flower's star-shaped petals in your nature journal.

*Ipomopsis aggregata*

### White fir

You may have seen this evergreen (keeps its leaves) tree in homes or other buildings. That's because the white fir is a popular choice for a Christmas tree. Look closely at its long, whitish blue needles. Crush one of them. Does it smell like tangerine to you? Rub it on your wrist for some fir cologne or perfume.

*Abies concolor* ("of the same color" in Latin)

### California kingsnake

This nonvenomous reptile gets its name because it does occasionally eat other snakes, like a king of the desert. The kingsnake is even immune to rattlesnake venom! You might spot one in the leaves or near the river, so keep an eye out when exploring. They have a beautiful striped pattern on their scales. Try to sketch it in your nature journal if you spot one.

*Lampropeltis californiae*

### Pineywoods geranium

This flower can range from bright pink to purple. It has five petals with dark veins running through them. If the petals are bending back toward the ground, that means it's in full bloom! Look for it May through September. Look closely. Can you spot the hairs on the petals? Does it have more or fewer hairs than on your arm?

*Geranium caespitosum*

# 33

# PEEK OVER THE EDGE AT TIMBER CREEK OVERLOOK

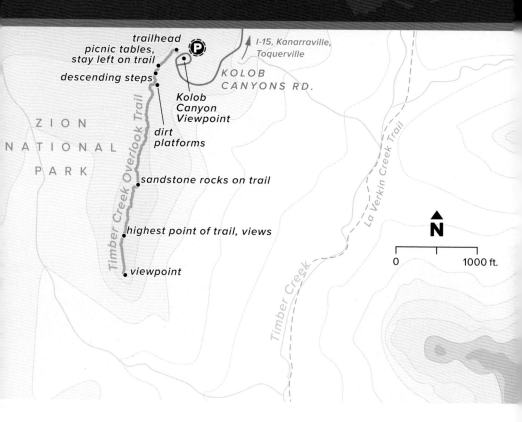

# YOUR ADVENTURE

Adventurers, today you're on the historical homelands of the Pueblo and Southern Paiute in Kolob Canyons, box canyons cutting into the Colorado Plateau and forming huge 2000-foot cliff walls. This trail starts off by going up dirt steps. Before long, you'll reach picnic tables. Stay to the left to continue hiking. You'll come across man-made dirt platforms you can hike on

This trek offers an incredible view of Kolob Canyons and Timber Creek →

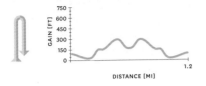

**LENGTH** 1.2 miles out and back

**ELEVATION GAIN** 269 ft.

**HIKE + EXPLORE** 1.5 hours

**DIFFICULTY** Moderate—relatively short but uphill most of the way in

**SEASON** Year-round. Springtime boasts amazing wildflowers. Snowy in the winter with potential road closures depending on snowfall; check for closures posted on the Zion National Park website under "Alerts in Effect." In winter will need proper footwear (snowshoes or spikes).

Summer gets hot, with possible wildfire smoke and afternoon showers.

**GET THERE** From I-15N, take Exit 40 toward Kolob Canyons. Turn right onto E Kolob Canyons Road. Drive for 5 miles to the Timber Creek Overlook Trail.

Google Maps: bit.ly/timbercreekoverlooktrail

**RESTROOMS** Yes

**FEE** $35 or free with annual pass

**TREAT YOURSELF** Stop and get a yummy smoothie from Kanarra Falls Snackery, about 11 miles north in Kanarraville.

Zion National Park
(435) 772-3256
Facebook @ZionNPS
zion_park_information@nps.gov
www.nps.gov/zion/index.htm

or around; they are here to divert rainwater to prevent the trail from flooding. The trail continues at a decent incline and will start to be covered with large sandstone rocks. Enjoy the view from the hike's highest point and then hike down to reach the lookout—you're almost there! The lookout has a beautiful view of Kolob Canyons and Timber Creek below, which meets up with La Verkin Creek and eventually flows into the Virgin River. Imagine these powerful creeks and rivers slowly carving these amazing canyons over time. Power up here and then hike back the way you came.

# SCAVENGER HUNT

### Juniper

This evergreen (doesn't lose its leaves) tree has different leaves than a pine tree. Look closely and see if you can spot its scales, much like a reptile's. Junipers also have small blueish berries, but don't eat them! They are actually modified cones just like on a pine tree. Its bark can break off in strips as well. If you find a strip on the ground, make a juniper bark bracelet out of it! These adaptive trees can live to be thousands of years old. How old do you think this one is?

*Juniperus* sp.

### Hairy false goldenaster

This plant gets its name from the gray hairs on the leaves and stems. Butterflies are attracted to its pretty yellow flowers that bloom from May to October. It grows best in sandy soil and in full sun. Can you spot it in those kinds of conditions?

*Heterotheca villosa*

### Sego lily

This is Utah's state flower. Native peoples showed Utah's early pioneers how to eat the sego lily's nutritious bulbs. After a cricket infestation reduced other food options, pioneers used this new knowledge, harvesting and eating the plants to survive. Do you think you could survive eating just flower bulbs?

*Calochortus nuttallii*

### Red-tailed hawk

This raptor (bird that eats prey) is the largest of all hawks. Its eyesight is eight times as powerful as a human's! This helps them see small rodents on the ground while they are flying high up in the sky. Put your arms out and glide along the trail, looking down to see if you can spot any ants. Listen for their strong *screech* call above you. Fun fact: The hawk screech you hear in movies is almost always the red-tailed hawk!

*Buteo jamaicensis*

### Armchair rock

When you get to the lookout point, scan your eyes over to the large rocks to your left. These were pushed up from the Hurricane Fault in the rock over

millions of years. If you look closely on the right side, you will see a large rock formation that looks like an armchair. How big do you think it is compared to your armchairs at home?

A chair in the hillside made of Navajo Sandstone, a sedimentary rock

# 34

# WIGGLE YOUR WAY UP TO THE WATCHMAN

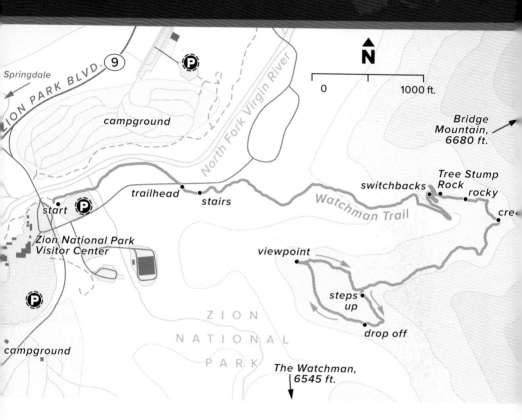

## YOUR ADVENTURE

Adventurers, today you're on the historical homelands of the Ancestral Puebloans and Parowan Fremont. You'll begin walking along the 162-mile-long Virgin River, which meets up with the massive 1450-mile-long Colorado River nearby. To get to the trailhead, you'll go through the parking lot and cross the road. Rock stairs slowly lead you up to switchbacks, as you

The 6545-foot-tall Watchman guards the valley →

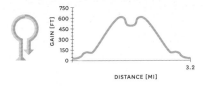

**LENGTH** 3.2-mile lollipop loop

**ELEVATION GAIN** 640 ft.

**HIKE + EXPLORE** 2.5 hours

**DIFFICULTY** Challenging—a heart-pumper perfect for getting your older or more experienced hikers used to more challenging ascents; trail starts out flat, then goes up with switchbacks for a mile or so, then levels out a bit for the last section; exposed section, so be careful with littles

**SEASON** Year-round. Can get muddy after rain. Trail is almost completely sun exposed, so plan for morning or late afternoon on hot days. Spring brings wildflowers and temperatures warm up. Fall offers lovely colors and slightly smaller crowds. Winter brings cooler weather and snow (roads are plowed) but some trails may be closed because of ice; be sure to check.

**GET THERE** Take UT-9E/Zion Park Blvd. to the Zion Canyon Visitor Center's parking lot. The trailhead is just before the parking lot; follow signs for the Watchman. The Zion National Park shuttle also stops here if you are coming from another part of the park or one of the stops in Springdale.

Google Maps: bit.ly/timberwatchman

**RESTROOMS** Yes

**FEE** $35 or free with annual pass

**TREAT YOURSELF** Hoodoos General Store and Ice Cream Parlor in Springdale has plenty of flavors to cool you off after your hard work.

Zion National Park
(435) 772-3256
Facebook @ZionNPS

look at Bridge Mountain looming above. Pass Tree Stump Rock, switchback again, and then begin to head up a rocky section. You'll pass a small creek, then the trail flattens out a bit. Finally you'll reach your first view of the Watchman. Plenty of rocky outcrops offer stops to power up or eat lunch on. Keep going and head counterclockwise on the loop on the mesa (an area of land that is flat-topped)—it curves down and around with a great view of the Watchman and Zion Canyon. Take it all in, complete the loop, and then head back the way you came. Of course, consider camping at the Watchman Campground to make it a full Watchman-themed day! Don't forget to get your stamp and Junior Ranger badge at the Zion Canyon Visitor Center when you're done.

# SCAVENGER HUNT

### Watchman Spire

Look at the layers of the different geological formations that make up the Watchman. The study of rock layers is called stratigraphy. Each layer tells a story about when it was deposited long ago. Can you tell which is the oldest formation, formed about 210 million years ago? You can find dinosaur tracks in this layer!

The Watchman's nine geological layers that rise 2200 feet in the air

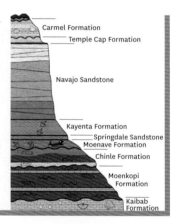

Carmel Formation
Temple Cap Formation
Navajo Sandstone
Kayenta Formation
Springdale Sandstone
Moenave Formation
Chinle Formation
Moenkopi Formation
Kaibab Formation

### Gray aster

Look for these small purple delights blooming in the spring. Gray asters clump up with each other. How many you can spot in one cluster? Then zoom in and count how many petals are on an individual flower.

*Herrickia glauca* ("bluish gray" in Latin)

## Mule deer

These majestic mammals munch around the Watchman in the cool mornings and evenings. You may see their small tracks heading off of the main trail. Look for their huge mule ears, which are used to help dissipate heat during long days in the Zion sun. What else might large ears help with?

*Odocoileus hemionus*

## Prickly pear cactus

There are four species of these succulents (plants that have fleshy tissues that hold water) in Zion. They are dormant in the winter, as they are unable to take in water from the cold ground, but then actively grow in the summer. Look for the yellow blooms in summer on their round pads. Take a whiff. What does it smell like? Once the blooms fade, their pink fruits called tuna will emerge.

*Opuntia* sp.

## California condor

Look for the largest flying land bird in North America! They have a 9.5-foot wingspan. Spread your arms out. How big is your wingspan—the length from the tip of one hand to the other? At the viewpoint, look for small black dots coasting on thermals, rising warm air pockets, around the Watchman. They almost disappeared from our planet in 1982, with only 22 left in the world. Now, thanks to the help of people like national park rangers, they are doing much better. Consider yourself lucky if you spot one!

*Gymnogyps californianus* (*gymnos* is Greek for "naked"—a nod to its bald head)

# 35

# RAILWALK TO ZION CANYON OVERLOOK

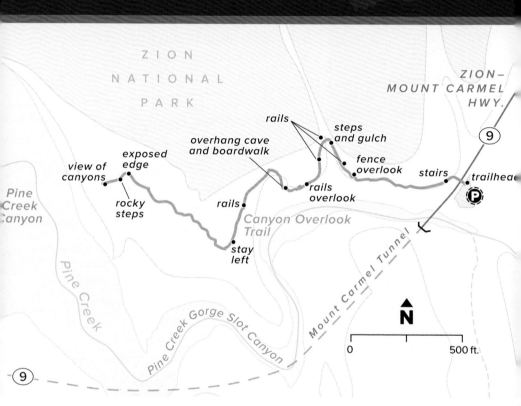

## YOUR ADVENTURE

Adventurers, today you're on the historical homelands of the Ancestral Puebloans and Parowan Fremont. You'll start by heading straight up the rock—hang on to the rails and you'll be fine! Power up at the top and then continue, being careful of the drop to Pine Creek on your left. You'll reach an overlook protected by a fence; check this out, and continue to follow

Cross the boardwalk to reach the overlook →

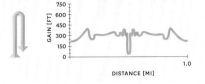

**LENGTH** 1.0 mile out and back

**ELEVATION GAIN** 430 ft.

**HIKE + EXPLORE** 1 hour

**DIFFICULTY** Moderate—several exposed edges with rails, stairs, sand, and rocky steps, and even a bridge above the canyon; short, but varied terrain and safety concerns

**SEASON** Year-round. Spring brings wildflowers and temperatures warm up. The summer is warm, so be sure to bring plenty of water, sun protection, and hike early or later in the day. Fall offers lovely colors and fewer people in the park. Winter brings cooler weather and snow (roads are plowed), but some trails may be closed because of ice; be sure to check.

**GET THERE** Take UT-9E/Zion Park Blvd. for 6 miles past the Zion Canyon Visitor Center. You will go through the 1.1-mile-long Mount Carmel Tunnel. The trailhead is on the left at the end of the tunnel. The first parking section is directly across from it on your right, but is super small. Fear not, just keep going and you'll find more on the left and right. You'll just need to walk a little bit to the trailhead.

Google Maps: bit.ly/timberzioncanyon

**RESTROOMS** Yes, just up the road at the next parking lot

**FEE** $35 or free with annual pass

**TREAT YOURSELF** Springdale Candy Company has rows and rows of goodies. Grab a bag, and snack at the viewpoint.

Zion National Park
(435) 772-3256
Facebook @ZionNPS

the rails around, up and down, until you cross a bridge over a gulch. You'll continue past more rails and reach a huge overhang and cave. Follow the trail around, stepping over rocks, and pass a narrow, mini V-shaped gorge. Be careful on the exposed ledge. Soon, you'll find yourself at the overlook! You are actually standing on top of Great Arch—perch on a small boulder to enjoy the view. When you're done, carefully head back the way you came. Get your stamp and Junior Ranger badge at the visitor center, and consider camping at Watchman Campground.

## SCAVENGER HUNT

### Fremont cottonwood

This deciduous (loses its leaves every year) tree blooms in March and April, producing a cluster of flowers in a 6-inch-long drooping shape called a cat-

kin. The leaves turn bright yellow in the fall. See how many of the spade-shaped leaves from the ground you can collect. Hand your bouquet to someone you love.

*Populus fremontii* leaves and catkin

### View

Imagine you're the Virgin River, carving through rock to create the canyon you see below. Can you see the two canyons—Pine Creek and Zion? Look for each of these peaks: the Sentinel (7120 feet); the Streaked Wall; the Altar of Sacrifice

West Temple    Altar of Sacrifice

(7505 feet); the West Temple (7810 feet); and Bridge Mountain on the left (6803 feet). Do you see another peak you could name?

At the viewpoint, how many of the landforms in the canyon can you spot?

### Sonoran scrub oak

Look for these sharply pointed leaves on the deciduous scrub oak. How many teeth do you count on just one leaf? Trace one in your natural journal. *Turbinella* means "spinning top." If you can find an acorn of this scrub oak, does that give you a clue to why botanists chose this name for it?

*Quercus turbinella*

### Desert bighorn sheep

These mammals love the east side of the tunnel right next to this trail! Look for them hopping along the cliffsides. July through October is bighorn mating season, also called the rut. You might see little lambs, who are born 6 months later, in the winter or spring. Do your best rock-hop sheep impersonation along the trail.

*Ovis canadensis nelsoni*

### Zion–Mount Carmel Tunnel

The 1.1-mile tunnel you just zoomed through was quite the feat to build back when it opened in 1928. Four crews worked for almost three years,

with people drilling and blasting from each end, to open Zion's beauty to visitors. This connected the park and the east, allowing visitors to drive directly into Zion Canyon. Give thanks to the teams who made your drive easy through the tunnel. Have you ever worked at something for three whole years?

A historical photo of the tunnel

# 36

# GO SPELUNKING IN THE LAVA TUBES

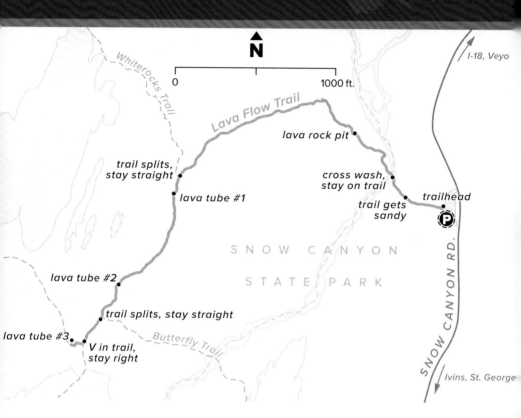

## YOUR ADVENTURE

Explorers, today you are on the historical homelands of the Southern Paiute, where you can do some cave exploration, also known as spelunking! The trail starts off flat among the red and white Navajo Sandstone of Snow Canyon, then you'll cross over a wash and continue on the trail. It will get rocky, so watch your step. Soon you will come to the first lava tube—it looks like a hole

These lava rocks hint at something fun underground →

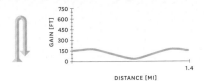

**LENGTH** 1.4 miles out and back

**ELEVATION GAIN** 184 ft.

**HIKE + EXPLORE** 2.5 hours

**DIFFICULTY** Moderate—easy downhill slope to the lava tubes, with lots of lava rock on the trail; hiking back is a bit tiring since it's a slight incline most of the way

**SEASON** Year-round. Very hot in the summer and the trail has no shade, so do it early in the morning or in the evening.

**GET THERE** From St. George, drive 11 miles north on UT-18. Turn left on Snow Canyon Drive to enter the state park, and after 1 mile the road to the Lava Flow Trailhead will be on the right.

Google Maps: bit.ly/timberlavatube

**RESTROOMS** At Upper and Lower Galoot Picnic Areas, 0.5 mile south of the Lava Flow Trailhead

**FEE** $10 per vehicle (Utah residents); $15 per vehicle (out-of-state visitors)

**TREAT YOURSELF** You can't miss stopping at Nielsen's Frozen Custard, about 10 miles south in St. George.

Snow Canyon State Park
(435) 628-2255
Facebook @UtahStateParks
Instagram @SnowCanyonStatePark

in the ground off to the right, but you'll see an informational sign by it. Careful, as there are no railings. You can climb down and explore, but this one is a bit tricky to navigate. As you continue hiking, you'll come to the next lava tube on your left. This one is mostly closed off but it's still fun to poke around on the lava rock. The trail will descend and you'll come to the third, largest lava tube. This is a great one to explore. It gets dark quickly, though, so turn your headlamps or flashlights on! After you're done exploring and powering up in the shade of the cave, make your way back the way you came.

# SCAVENGER HUNT

## Lava rock

Do you notice how most of the rocks on the trail are black? That's because they are lava rock! These rocks were once part of the inside of the Earth and were ejected by the nearby Santa Clara Volcano long ago. As the molten lava cooled, it formed into these igneous (cooled from lava) basalt rocks. Sketch what you think it looked like when the cinder cones erupted. Would you want to have been on the trail?

Cooled magma from around 15,000 years ago

## Silver cholla

This succulent (plant that keeps water in its flesh) gets its name from its silvery spines. Do you see how they shine? If you're visiting in the spring or summer, you might be lucky to see some yellow flowers blooming among the spines. Birds like to build their nests in the branches, where they are safe from predators. Does it look like a place where you'd like to build your home?

*Cylindropuntia echinocarpa*, echino means "hedgehog" in Greek

### Bats

Keep an eye out for bats in the lava tubes. You might find big and little brown bats hanging upside down to rest. Their talons lock in and it doesn't take them any energy to hang like that. Do you think you could sleep upside down?

Several species of bats roost in the lava tubes

### Lava tubes

Lava tubes are natural channels that hot lava once traveled through like a river, beneath the surface of the ground. After the flow of lava from an eruption stops, it leaves behind large empty caves, like the ones you get to explore on this trail. Exploring caves lets you see a whole new world—just don't forget your headlamp or flashlight!

Opening to the third lava tube

### Greater roadrunner

While they *can* fly, these birds usually stick to running. Roadrunners usually travel at speeds of around 15 miles per hour, but can have fast sprints up to 25 miles per hour! They like to run because their prey—ranging from snakes to scorpions to frogs—lives on the ground. As you might notice, there isn't a lot of water in the desert. Roadrunners are well adapted and quench their thirst with the foods they eat. What is an adaptation you have in the heat? Sprint to the next spot on the trail, and share how many miles per hour you think you went!

*Geococcyx californianus*

# ADVENTURES IN
# NEVADA

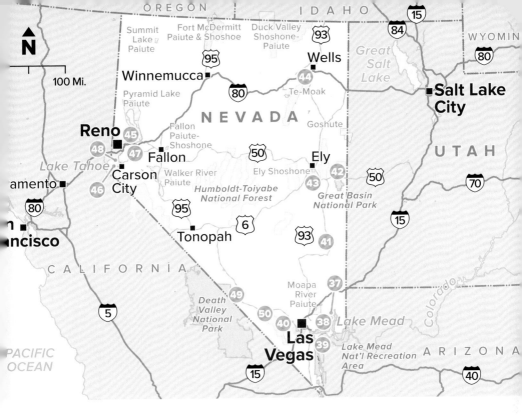

*Adventurers,* welcome to the Silver State, which joined the United States in 1864. You'll explore huge, white domes, read ancient petroglyphs in Valley of Fire State Park, walk through historic tunnels near Lake Mead, find some old water tanks at Red Rock Canyon National Conservation Area, and check out the tall, drippy canyons and caves of Cathedral Gorge State Park. You'll drive a bit on the "Loneliest Road in America," US Route 50, before arriving at the Ward Charcoal Ovens State Historic Park, part of Nevada's rich mining past. Explore the Alpine Lakes of Great Basin National Park, and continue north to Smith Lake. Catch I-80 and land yourself in the Reno area, where you can explore the Griffith Canyon petroglyphs, watch wildlife around Spooner Lake, see the ruins of Fort Churchill, and explore Monkey Rock. End by visiting an old ghost town in Rhyolite or loop back to Mount Charleston for Mary Jane Falls. Let's embrace the state motto, "All for Our Country," and explore as much of Nevada as we can!

# 37

# WALK BETWEEN THE WHITE DOMES

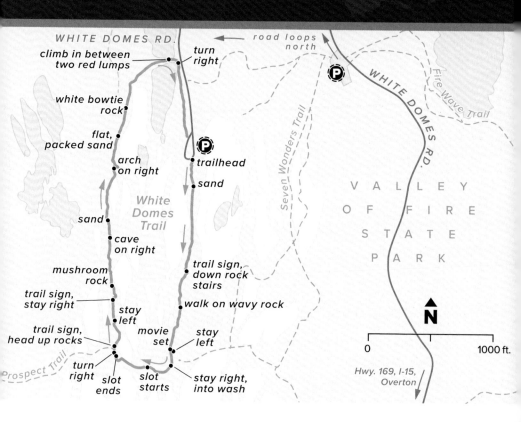

WHITE DOMES RD.

climb in between
two red lumps

turn
right

road loops
north

white bowtie
rock

flat,
packed sand

arch
on right

trailhead

sand

sand

White
Domes
Trail

cave
on right

mushroom
rock

trail sign,
stay right

trail sign,
down rock
stairs

stay
left

walk on wavy rock

trail sign,
head up rocks

movie
set

stay
left

Prospect Trail

turn
right

slot
ends

slot
starts

stay right,
into wash

Seven Wonders Trail

Fire Wave Trail

WHITE DOMES RD.

V A L L E Y
O F   F I R E
S T A T E
P A R K

**N**

0                    1000 ft.

Hwy. 169, I-15,
Overton

# YOUR ADVENTURE

Adventurers, today you're on the historical homelands of the Ancestral
Puebloans and Southern Paiute in the Mojave Desert, among red sandstone
that once was vast sand dunes during the time of the dinosaurs 150 million
years ago. Begin walking between the two huge white domes on sand, until

The trail is sandy among the massive white rock domes →

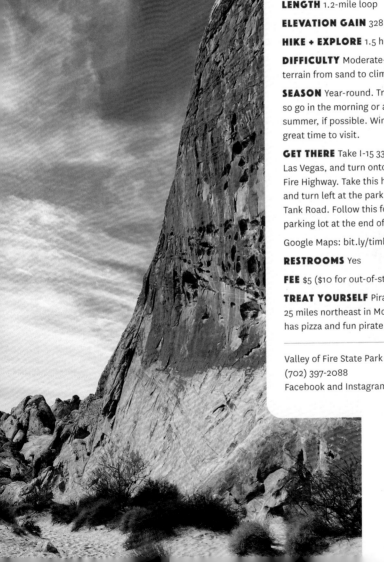

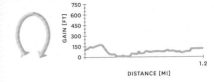

GAIN [FT]

750
600
450
300
150
0

1.2

DISTANCE [MI]

**LENGTH** 1.2-mile loop

**ELEVATION GAIN** 328 ft.

**HIKE + EXPLORE** 1.5 hours

**DIFFICULTY** Moderate—a mix of terrain from sand to climbing rocks

**SEASON** Year-round. Trail is fully exposed, so go in the morning or afternoon and avoid summer, if possible. Winter is cool and a great time to visit.

**GET THERE** Take I-15 33 miles north of Las Vegas, and turn onto Exit 75 for Valley of Fire Highway. Take this highway for 18 miles, and turn left at the park entrance on Mouse's Tank Road. Follow this for 5.6 miles to the parking lot at the end of the road.

Google Maps: bit.ly/timberdomes

**RESTROOMS** Yes

**FEE** $5 ($10 for out-of-state plates)

**TREAT YOURSELF** Pirates Landing, 25 miles northeast in Moapa Valley, has pizza and fun pirate decor.

Valley of Fire State Park
(702) 397-2088
Facebook and Instagram @Valley.of.Fire

you reach rock steps that take you down to a former movie set. Do your best movie acting and continue on to the left, where you'll then go through rocky Kaolin Wash and come upon White Domes slot. Wind in and out until you emerge on the other side of the canyon, where you'll follow a trail sign to the right. Here, the trail opens up to expansive views of the valley, with white, yellow, and red rocks all around you. Pass by an arch, then follow a trail sign to the right and squeeze between two red lumps. Walk past the so-called Indian Marbles, rocks that have freed themselves from the erosion. Follow the road back to where you started. Be sure to check out the visitor center and fill out their phenology/sightings board. Consider camping at the Atlatl Rock Campground by the entrance to extend the fun in this magical place.

# SCAVENGER HUNT

### Catclaw acacia

The seeds of this deciduous (loses its leaves) tree form pods in the late

summer and fall. It's called catclaw because of its hooked thorns. This acacia is also called the wait-a-minute bush, because if you walk through one you'll have to wait a minute while you dethorn yourself! The leaves are pinnate, meaning they are split with perfect opposites. How many leaves can you count on one branch?

*Senegalia greggii*

### Common side-blotched lizard

Look for the dark and light spotted pattern on this reptile's back as it darts across the trail. If you're quiet, you might be able to get close enough for your own photo. Males are a bit more colored than females, with bright blue speckling on their tail, back, and back limbs.

*Uta stansburiana*

### Slot canyon

The canyon walls narrow through this section of the trail—enjoy squeezing through it. You're walking through the Aztec Sandstone (very similar to the Navajo Sandstone in Utah) that's 180 million years old. Imagine rain coming down but not absorbing into the hard, dry sand. Where could it go? It can only rush toward the canyon in powerful flash floods, carving the swirls that you walk through in the canyon today.

The Narrows

### Movie set

Check out where the famous 1966 western *The Professionals* was shot, along with eleven other movies! That movie set featured a Mexican hacienda (house). Can you still see the wooden beams? Keep your eyes peeled for railroad ties on the ground as well. What kind of movie would you shoot here? Write a plot in your nature journal.

An old film set

### Utah yucca

When this plant flowers in spring, its single flower stalk can grow up to 5 feet tall! Is it taller than you today? Yuccas like growing in clumps with others in the sand. Their sharp pointy leaves narrow to help water slide right down to the base of the plant—an adaptation that allows them to live in this harsh, dry environment.

*Yucca utahensis*

# 38

# PEEP THE PETROGLYPHS AT MOUSE'S TANK

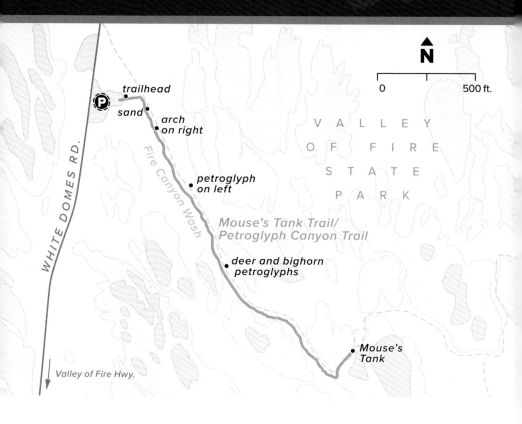

# YOUR ADVENTURE

Adventurers, today you're on the historical homelands of the Basketmaker people. Begin by heading down the concrete path that leads you into the sand. You'll be walking in Petroglyph Canyon between two rock structures. Keep your eyes peeled for the black varnish that shines. When you see it, be on the alert for petroglyphs made by Native Americans—some of them

Ready to go petroglyph hunting? →

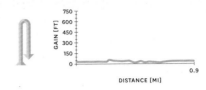

750
600
450
300
150
0
GAIN [FT]

0.9
DISTANCE [MI]

**LENGTH** 0.9 miles out and back

**ELEVATION GAIN** 56 ft.

**HIKE + EXPLORE** 1 hour

**DIFFICULTY** Easy—a flat and fairly smooth trail

**SEASON** Year-round. Trail is exposed, so be sure to take precautions on warm days—bring a hat, extra water, and avoid the heat of midday. Winter is a great time to explore the park without the heat.

**GET THERE** Take I-15 33 miles north of Las Vegas, and turn onto Exit 75 for Valley of Fire Highway. Take this highway 18 miles to Mouse's Tank Road and turn left. The parking lot will be on your right in 1.1 miles.

Google Maps: bit.ly/timberpetroglyph

**RESTROOMS** Yes

**FEE** $5 ($10 for out-of-state plates)

**TREAT YOURSELF** Treat the whole family to the Tournament of Kings dinner theater at the Excalibur Hotel at the south end of the Strip in Las Vegas.

Valley of Fire State Park
(702) 397-2088
Facebook and Instagram @Valley.of.Fire

more than 4000 years old! The first set will be on your left—the two best friends. Next, you'll walk a bit to the left for a better view of an enormous rock on which the petroglyph carvers really had a party. Next, you'll find some images really high up to the left—including deer and bighorn sheep. Go up into a cave to the right and you'll find some etched on the brown rock itself. Continue on, and you'll see a sign directing you to the end of the trail on the left, where you can look down into Mouse's Tank. Turn back the way you came, and consider camping at the nearby campground.

# SCAVENGER HUNT

### Paddlewheel petroglyph

Heading in, be sure to look under the cove on the right side of the trail to see this collection of petroglyphs. The dark portion of the rock is called desert varnish. It's made of clay, sand grains, metal oxides, and other elements. Bacteria take some oxides out of the environment, add oxygen, and cement it onto rock surfaces. Desert varnish comes from atmospheric dust and surface runoff, so streaks of black varnish often appear where water falls over cliffs. You can recreate petroglyphs at home by covering a piece of paper with a crayon and scratching through it with your fingernail or a key.

A paddlewheel among the petroglyphs

Person

Person
with shield

antelope /
sheep / elk

centipede

### Shaman petroglyph

Archaeologists study the past through clues left by ancient peoples, like

these petroglyphs. This shape is suspected to represent a shaman or medicine person, like a modern-day doctor. What else do you see here? Eric John Pacl from the University of Nevada put together a study of the petroglyphs in the Valley of Fire and codified all the different ones he saw. Try to draw your own in your nature journal!

These look like two best friends.

### Sheep petroglyph

These petroglyphs date back 2000 to 4000 years. How many storms have they seen? It's miraculous they're still visible. The difference between a petroglyph and a pictograph is that a petroglyph is etched *into* the rock and a pictograph is painted *on* a rock. More than 150 sheep images are recorded in the Valley of Fire, showing how important they were to the people who lived here.

The height of petroglyphs indicated what category they were; in the middle are hunting and cultivating scenes.

### Mouse's Tank

Mouse's Tank is a basin in the rock where water collects after rainfall. A Southern Paiute named Little Mouse hid out in the Valley of Fire for several years in the 1890s, after he was accused of crimes in the area. What makes this spot a good hideout?

Mouse's Tank basin

# 39

# WALK THROUGH HISTORY IN THE OLD RAILROAD TUNNEL

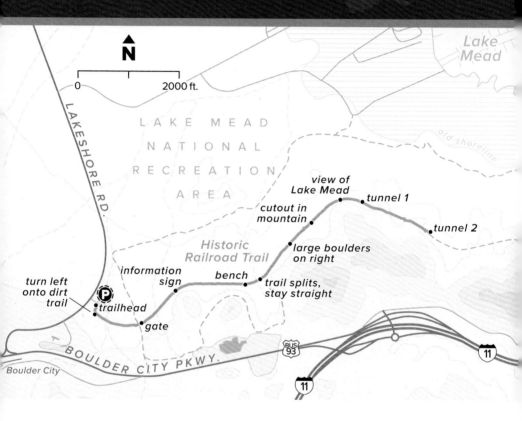

## YOUR ADVENTURE

Adventurers, today you're on the historical homelands of the Chemehuevi in the River Mountains. This trail runs over the old railroad used to haul equipment to build Hoover Dam. The trail starts on a paved sidewalk but quickly makes a left onto a dirt trail. You'll hike through a large open gate and continue on the wide gravel trail, passing a bench where you can power

Take a walk along Lake Mead on the Historic Railroad Trail →

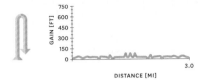

**LENGTH** 3.0 miles out and back

**ELEVATION GAIN** 29 ft.

**HIKE + EXPLORE** 2.5 hours

**DIFFICULTY** Easy—a flat trail that is wide, well maintained, and easy to navigate

**SEASON** Year-round. Best in late fall, winter, early spring. The summer temperatures can be extreme; even in the spring and fall, it's best to go in the morning or evening. Be aware of snakes on the trail in the spring and fall.

**GET THERE** From Boulder City, take Route 93 for 2.4 miles. Turn left onto Lakeshore Road, and the second right leads to the parking lot for the trailhead.

Google Maps: bit.ly/timberrailroadtunnel

**RESTROOMS** Yes

**FEE** None

**TREAT YOURSELF** After your hike, stop by Southwest Diner, 5 miles south in Boulder City, and get a homemade meal with a slice of pie on the side.

Lake Mead National Recreation Area
(702) 293-8990
Facebook @LakeMeadNPS

up if it gets too hot and pass a trail to your right—stay straight here. You'll have a beautiful view of Lake Mead on your left. Continue on this wide trail as it winds around through the hills. After about half a mile, you'll see that the trail looks like it has cut its way right through the hills. You'll come to the first tunnel. Inside, you might be lucky enough to hear bats. The second tunnel still has an old shipping container inside; you need to walk through to get out the other end. Power up here in the shade, then head back the way you came.

# SCAVENGER HUNT

### Bighorn sheep

Look high up the mountain and you might be lucky enough to see one of these hooved mammals. Their large horns can weigh as much as 30 pounds.

That's like carrying almost four gallons of milk on your head! The males use their horns to show status to other bighorn sheep and for fighting. Females have horns as well and use them to defend themselves and their lambs against predators. Find two sticks and make your own horns by your head.

*Ovis canadensis*

### Mexican free-tailed bat

These bats migrate to this area every year. If you are visiting between May and October, you will probably be lucky enough to hear or even see these small mammals. They love to hang out in the tunnel crevices and from the wooden beams. Can you hear their little squeaks?

*Tadarida brasiliensis*

### Creosote bush

This desert plant has to work hard to grow in harsh conditions. Since there isn't much water, the creosote bush has adapted to efficiently absorb any water it can, even if that means stealing. It's so good at absorbing all the water that seeds from other plants in the area are not able to get any and can't germinate or begin to grow. Look for its pretty yellow flowers in the spring and take a whiff. What does it smell like to you?

*Larrea tridentata* ("three-toothed" in Latin— a reference to its leaves)

### Railroad tunnel

The railroad was used to carry materials to build the Hoover Dam. Trains ran 24 hours a day carrying gravel, supplies, and machinery to the construction site. The tunnels were built in just 5 months in 1931, carved right through the hillside so the trains could get through. The second tunnel has wooden beams in it to help reinforce the tunnel so the rock wouldn't fracture and fall. Can you imagine using a jackhammer out in 100-degree weather to build a tunnel?

Tunnel carved through the mountain

# 40

# SCRAMBLE OVER RED ROCKS UP TO CALICO TANKS

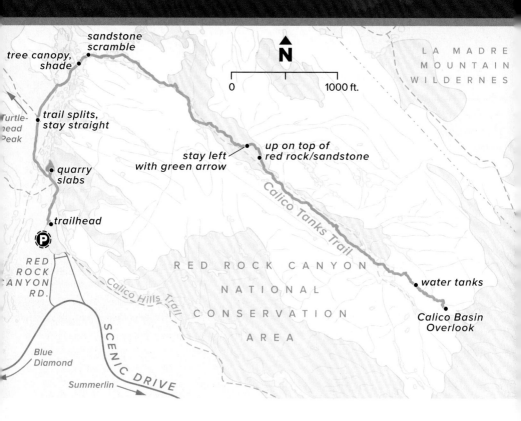

## YOUR ADVENTURE

Adventurers, today we're exploring the homelands of the Southern Paiute among the Calico Hills, an area that was red sand dunes 180 million years ago. Begin on a gravel trail, and you'll come to an open area and follow the sign with the green arrow to the trail. But wait! Make sure to take a look at the huge slabs of white sandstone cut from the wall—then continue on

This hike offers a great view of Red Rock Canyon →

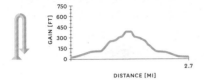

**LENGTH** 2.7 miles out and back

**ELEVATION GAIN** 427 ft.

**HIKE + EXPLORE** 3 hours

**DIFFICULTY** Challenging—scrambling on sandstone is fun, but it adds an element of difficulty

**SEASON** Year-round. Best in spring, fall, winter. Summer temperatures can be extreme, it's best to go in the morning or late afternoon. Spring and fall are good for wildflowers and migrating birds, and summer brings out lizards. Be reptile-aware: Look before you sit down, and don't reach into rocks or areas that you can't see.

**GET THERE** From Las Vegas, follow 215W and take Exit 26 for Charleston Blvd./NV-159. Turn right (west) onto Charleston Blvd. Continue for 5 miles. Turn right onto Red Rock Canyon Scenic Loop Drive. Follow the signs and make a slight right onto Scenic Loop Dr. Drive for 2.5 miles and turn into the third pullout called Sandstone Quarry. Timed entry reservations from Recreation .gov are required from May to October.

Google Maps: bit.ly/timbercalicotanks

**RESTROOMS** Yes

**FEE** $20 or free with annual pass

**TREAT YOURSELF** If you're in the mood for some great breakfast food, stop at BabyStacks Cafe, 5 miles east, for many different varieties of pancakes.

Red Rock Canyon National Conservation Area
(702) 515-5350
Facebook @RedRockCanyonLV

the trail. Avoid the turnoff on your left for Turtlehead Peak and continue straight to Calico Tanks. Cross some dry washes and you'll arrive under a canopy of trees. You'll emerge in a small canyon with walls on either side. Once it opens up, this is the part where you get to use your hands! The trail will take you right up onto the sandstone—you have to climb up to keep going. Sandstone can be slippery, so wear good shoes and watch out for drops of water. The signs with green arrows will continue to guide you. After climbing up, you'll come to the tanks. Just past them, climb up to a beautiful overlook of Calico Basin. Return the way you came, and consider camping nearby at Red Rock Campground.

# SCAVENGER HUNT

### Quarry stones

Early on the hike, you'll come to the Excelsior Stone Quarry. These large blocks of white sandstone can weigh as much as 10 tons! The quarry was opened in 1905, and this sandstone was shipped to markets in San Francisco and Los Angeles, where it was carved into decorations for buildings. What would you build with these stones?

Blocks from the Excelsior Stone Quarry

### Cholla cactus

This prickly succulent (fleshy plant that holds water) has barbed spines, so be sure to look but do not touch! If you are hiking in spring, you might notice yellow or orange flowers. In addition to producing seeds, these cactuses spread by attaching parts of their branches to wildlife (and unwary hikers), so they'll fall off in different locations. If you were a cactus, what strategy would you use to spread?

*Cylindropuntia acanthocarpa*

### Water basin

It's rare to find large pools of water in the desert, but if there's enough rain, this water basin could be full! The tank provides water for wildlife, like bighorn sheep and frogs. Is it full today? It can run dry in the summer and fall. Do the Wildlife 5-Minute Challenge: Sit silently and see what wildlife visits the tank in 5 minutes!

Tanks are also called *tinajas*, Spanish for "earthen jar"

### Desert willow

These delicate pink or purple flowers are often seen after a rainstorm. So if it's rained within a few days of your hike, look out for these beauties! If you do see one, give it a whiff and touch its long, narrow leaves. Trace one in your nature journal.

*Chilopsis linearis* (*cheília* is Greek for "lips")

### Desert tortoise

The desert tortoise—the Nevada state reptile—has been on Earth for millions of years. It is an endangered species, so if you see one don't disturb it. The Red Rock Canyon Visitor Center has a habitat exhibit where they house rescued pet desert tortoises. Have a tortoise race with your hiking buddy; you have to go as slowly as possible.

*Gopherus agassizii*

# 41

# MOONWALK AND CAVEWALK AT CATHEDRAL GORGE

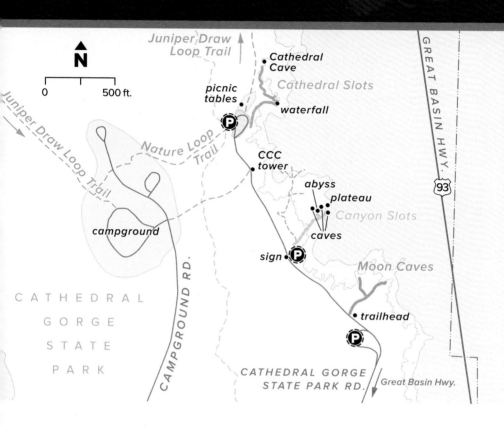

## YOUR ADVENTURE

Adventurers, today you're on the historical homelands of the Fremont and Paiute, exploring three different areas. Begin your journey at the Moon Caves sign. Zigzag your way in and hit a fork—go to the right first. You'll meander to a final cul-de-sac, where you can circle around a little rock feature. Head back to the fork, and turn left, where there is a tunnel on the ground!

Get ready to squeeze through Cathedral Gorge →

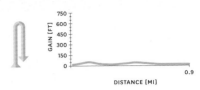

GAIN [FT]

750
600
450
300
150
0

0.9

DISTANCE [MI]

**LENGTH** 0.9 miles out and back

**ELEVATION GAIN** 30 ft.

**HIKE + EXPLORE** 1 hour

**DIFFICULTY** Challenging—a collection of three short trails (each 0.3 mile) that involves squeezing through slots and some light climbing; fairly flat but the trail can get very narrow and sandy

**SEASON** Year-round. Spring and fall are cooler and the best times to explore. If you come in the summer, be sure to bring plenty of water and consider hiking in the early or late hours. Winter can get chilly and road conditions can vary, while spring and fall offer pleasant temperatures.

**GET THERE** From Pioche, take Highway 93 7.3 miles south, turn right onto Cathedral Gorge State Park Road, and drive for 1.4 miles. Park in the pullout next to the sign for Moon Slots.

Google Maps: bit.ly/timbercathedral

**RESTROOMS** Yes, at the end by Cathedral Slots

**FEE** $5 ($10 for out-of-state plates)

**TREAT YOURSELF** Gunslingers, just 7 miles north in Pioche, offers milkshakes and more, perfect to cool off after exploring the gorge.

Cathedral Gorge State Park
(775) 728-8101
Facebook @CathedralGorgeStatePark2015

If you're brave, you can easily squeeze through. It opens to a new slot to explore, which eventually takes you to a rope climb—only adults or experienced climbers should try this. Head back to the beginning. Next, walk or drive to the Canyon Slots parking area. First take the entrance on the right, which goes straight back, with a little bit of climbing, and then forks to three different caves. Try the one on the right first, following the smoothest path up to the right to the mouth of the cave. Be careful—this one has a steep drop down, so hold hands here, lead adventurers! Head to the second cave and climb to reach the top of this formation. Head down again and make your way to the third cave on the left. Next, walk a bit farther down to the brown sign that says Canyon Slots. Turn right into the canyons, searching for the obvious opening. There's a split, so take the first one to the right where it dead ends. Go back to the fork, and then head down the slot until you reach a three-way fork and explore each one. Head back the way you came. Walk or drive along the road, passing by the CCC tower, and then reach your final slot adventure: the Cathedral Slots. Head straight in and hit a fork. Each side leads to two different dead ends/dry waterfalls. Head back the way you came and power up at the picnic tables. You can take the 0.5-mile Nature Loop to extend the fun. Stop off at the visitor center to get your State Park Passport Stamp! Consider staying at the campground in the park.

# SCAVENGER HUNT

### Caves

These caves are made of soft bentonite clay and were created by erosion, which occurs here from rainwater, melting snow, freezing and thawing cycles, and evaporation. Pile up a little mound of dirt at the entrance of the park and pour water on it—what happens?

Can you find the cave in the Canyon Slots?

## CCC projects

President Franklin D. Roosevelt created the Civilian Conservation Corps in the 1930s, during the Great Depression. The CCC hired workers who needed jobs to create some of the country's most magnificent outdoor structures. What are two things you notice about the way these are constructed?

Structures built in the 1930s

## Dry waterfall tube

This layer of rocks around you is called the Panaca Formation. This entire area was covered by a huge lake a million years ago. When the land began to uplift, the lake drained and revealed all this sediment. Volcanic activity from the Caliente Caldera Complex also continually deposited ash here in layers, and then water eroded the soft clay and siltstone away, leaving this maze of rocks. Look up some of these tall tubes. They were carved by the water!

Waterfalls once flowed here

## Desert cottontail rabbit

You might get lucky and see this small mammal with its little cotton-ball tail hopping around the desert. When you get home, draw a rabbit in your nature journal and glue a cotton ball from the bathroom to its tail. Cottontail rabbits are herbivores, eating any plant they can find, even cactus. What's your favorite vegetable?

*Sylvilagus audubonii*

# 42

# AMBLE ALONG TO TWO ALPINE LAKES

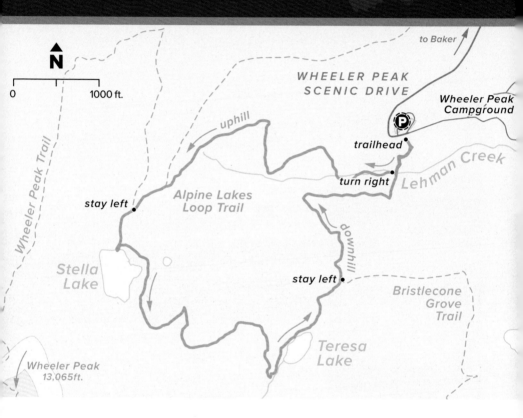

**N**

0    1000 ft.

to Baker

WHEELER PEAK
SCENIC DRIVE

Wheeler Peak
Campground

uphill

*trailhead*

Wheeler Peak Trail

*stay left*

Alpine Lakes
Loop Trail

*turn right*    Lehman Creek

downhill

Stella
Lake

*stay left*

Bristlecone
Grove
Trail

Teresa
Lake

Wheeler Peak
13,065ft.

## YOUR ADVENTURE

Adventurers, today you're on the historical homelands of the Goshute in the Snake Mountain Range. You'll begin in a forest, crossing Lehman Creek over a bridge and turning right on the Alpine Lakes Loop Trail. Continue and stay left to pass the Wheeler Peak Trail; soon you'll arrive at Stella Lake. Power up here in the high altitude and take in the excellent view of

Relax in this unique alpine atmosphere →

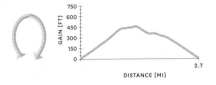

GAIN [FT] — DISTANCE [MI] — 2.7

**LENGTH** 2.7-mile loop

**ELEVATION GAIN** 472 ft.

**HIKE + EXPLORE** 2 hours

**DIFFICULTY** Challenging—the terrain is rocky, and hiking at 10,000 feet is more difficult, so be sure to wear sturdy shoes, take it slow, drink a lot of water, and eat

**SEASON** Wheeler Peak Road closes with the first snow and opens again in the spring, so check the national park website or call to make sure the road is open. The aspens turn a brilliant yellow in the fall.

**GET THERE** Take NV-488 4.8 miles west of Baker. Turn right onto Wheeler Peak Scenic Drive, which goes for 11.7 miles and ends at the parking lot.

Google Maps: bit.ly/timberalpine

**RESTROOMS** Yes

**FEE** None

**TREAT YOURSELF** Build your own burger or grilled cheese at the 487 Grill food cart in Baker.

Great Basin National Park
(775) 234-7331
Facebook @GreatBasinNPS

Wheeler Peak. Curve around down through the bumpy terrain left behind by the glacier and soon you'll be at Teresa Lake. Power up here and continue downhill back into the forest. You'll pass the Bristlecone Grove Trail on your right and soon arrive back at the parking lot. Make sure to stay right at the final junction. Head to the visitor center to get your Junior Ranger badge. Consider camping by the trailhead at Wheeler Peak Campground.

# SCAVENGER HUNT

### Mule deer

Be sure to walk quietly through the pine and aspen forest, so you don't scare away the mule deer that love it here. The males are called bucks and grow antlers, which first start out even and then grow randomly. Sketch antlers in your nature journal. Mule deer are best seen in the morning or evening.

*Odocoileus hemionus*

### Wheeler Peak

You'll get two awesome views of Wheeler Peak, the second-highest peak in Nevada. See if you can spot the three lobes of a rock glacier—kind of like a snow and ice glacier, but made of rocks that slowly glide down with ice and carve out the mountain—on top. Sketch the ridgeline in your nature journal. Can you find the horn of the peak?

Wheeler Peak reaches 13,065 feet

### Parry's primrose

In the summer, look for the bright magenta flowers of Parry's primrose. The plant bears up to twenty-five flowers on one stem popping up from bright, floppy, lance-shaped leaves at the base. Get up close and take a whiff. These flowers do *not* smell pleasant. What does it smell like to you?

*Primula parryi*

### Glacial lakes

Today you get to see a special kind of lake called a tarn. Tarns form from holes carved by glaciers that leave sediment behind, making the pool a beautiful turquoise color. Both of these alpine lakes are shallow (no deeper

than 20 feet), but Teresa Lake is fed by a spring—see if you can find it. In the summer, beautiful wildflowers bloom here. The rings around the lakes show how deep the water was in the past. Was it deeper in previous years based on what you see this year?

Teresa Lake (left) and Stella Lake (right)

### Clark's nutcracker

Look and listen for these songbirds in the treetops. They are gray, black, and white with a long, sharp, black bill used for ripping seeds out of pine cones. The birds stash the pine nuts under their tongue, and in summer they bury them in the ground to eat in winter. Hold some food under your tongue and pretend you had to hide it for the winter. What would that be like?

*Nucifraga columbiana*

# 43

# JAUNT THROUGH THE JUNIPERS TO THE CHARCOAL OVENS

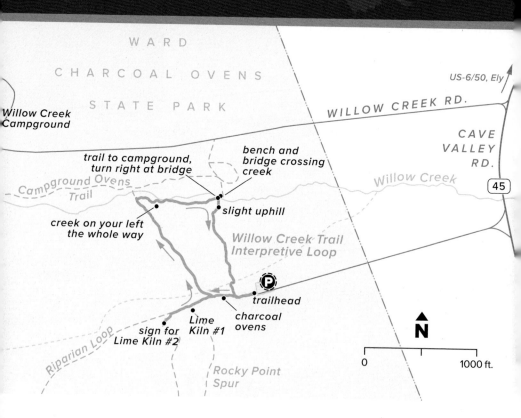

WARD

CHARCOAL OVENS

STATE PARK

US-6/50, Ely

Willow Creek
Campground

WILLOW CREEK RD.

CAVE
VALLEY
RD.

trail to campground,
turn right at bridge

bench and
bridge crossing
creek

Willow Creek

45

Campground Ovens
Trail

slight uphill

creek on your left
the whole way

Willow Creek Trail
Interpretive Loop

trailhead

charcoal
ovens

Lime
Kiln #1

sign for
Lime Kiln #2

Riparian Loop

N

Rocky Point
Spur

0          1000 ft.

## YOUR ADVENTURE

Adventurers, today you're on the historical homelands of the Western Shoshone in the Egan Mountain Range. You'll begin your journey walking right up to six charcoal ovens! Run inside each one. Can you imagine charcoal burning inside? Continue the journey just a few hundred feet up to the lime kilns on your left. Be sure to walk up the hillside to see Lime Kiln #1.

Explore inside these historic beehive-shaped ovens →

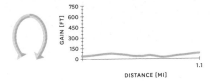

GAIN [FT]

750
600
450
300
150
0

1.1

DISTANCE [MI]

**LENGTH** 1.1-mile loop

**ELEVATION GAIN** 72 ft.

**HIKE + EXPLORE** 1 hour

**DIFFICULTY** Easy—a flat and fairly smooth trail

**SEASON** Year-round. In the winter, Cave Valley Road gets snow and may not be plowed, so call ahead. Trail can also get icy. Best in spring with cooler temps and Willow Creek at full flow.

**GET THERE** From Ely, take US-93S 5.6 miles south and turn right on Cave Valley Road, which is the first right after the big brown sign for Ward Charcoal Kilns State Park. Follow that for 9.9 miles, and turn right at the sign to reach the parking lot.

Google Maps: bit.ly/timberwardcharcoal

**RESTROOMS** Yes

**FEE** $5 ($10 for out-of-state plates)

**TREAT YOURSELF** Taproot in Ely offers banana splits and lots of different milkshake flavors, plus tasty coffee drinks for our lead adventurers.

Ward Charcoal Ovens State Historic Park
(775) 289-1693
Facebook @NVStateParks

Head back to the main trail, then turn right to go back to the charcoal ovens. Just where they begin, on your left there is a sign for Willow Creek. Take the Interpretive Loop Trail to the right of the sign (the left is an animal trail that doesn't connect). You'll begin winding through the pinyon pines and junipers. Soon you'll reach a bench—power up here and continue on to the next bench at Willow Creek. Keep going right (not toward the picnic tables) and follow the creek. You'll soon reach a small bridge over the creek, and then a trail that goes to the picnic tables and campground. Have lunch and power up here, and then head back to close the loop. Consider making a weekend of it at the campground in the park.

# SCAVENGER HUNT

### Willow Creek

Water is life. How much have you drunk today? Willow Creek is a spring that provided water for all the workers camping near and working in the kilns, and today it provides water and habitat for the wildlife of the park. Can you see any?

Willow Creek later meets up with South Fork Willow Creek

### Utah juniper

These evergreen (keep their leaves) trees were used as fuel for the charcoal ovens. When the number of trees left got too small, it signaled the end of the ovens' industry. Collect twenty blue juniper cones from the ground and give them a whiff. Then leave them so they can be a snack for the birds.

*Juniperus osteosperma*

### Lime kilns

These kilns are differently shaped than the beehive-shaped ovens at the beginning of the trail. These kilns were used to make lime mortar, which was then used to bond together the stones of the charcoal ovens! Imagine workers moving back and forth between the two sites.

Kilns burn lime at 900 celcius

### Charcoal ovens

These ovens were constructed in the 1870s and were only in operation for three years. They could fit thirty-five cords of wood. A cord is a stack of split wood 4 feet wide, 4 feet high, and 8 feet deep. That's a lot! Once in there, the wood burned for twelve full days and made fifty bushels of charcoal per cord. In turn, the charcoal was used as fuel to smelt the ore used in gold and silver mining nearby.

Charcoal oven

### Pronghorn

Antlers are bony structures that are usually only grown by males, shed and regrown each year. Horns are grown by both males and females and continue to grow through an animal's life. Pronghorns are special because they are the only animals to shed their horns. They're also the fastest animal in the Western Hemisphere! Look for pronghorn tracks, which are similar to a deer's.

*Antilocapra americana*

# 44

# SWITCHBACK UP TO SMITH LAKE

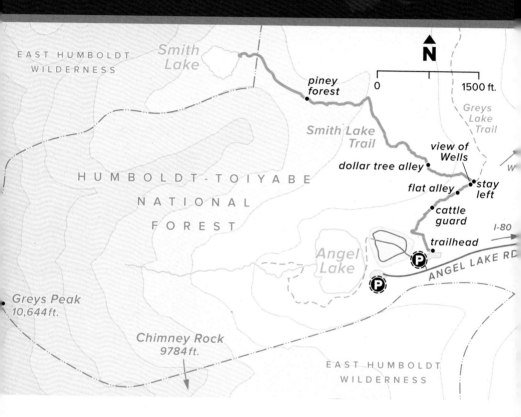

**EAST HUMBOLDT WILDERNESS**

Smith Lake

piney forest

Smith Lake Trail

dollar tree alley

N

0        1500 ft.

Greys Lake Trail

view of Wells

flat alley

stay left

cattle guard

W

HUMBOLDT-TOIYABE NATIONAL FOREST

trailhead

I-80

Angel Lake

ANGEL LAKE RD

Greys Peak 10,644 ft.

Chimney Rock 9784 ft.

EAST HUMBOLDT WILDERNESS

## YOUR ADVENTURE

Adventurers, today you're on the historical homelands of the Western Shoshone in the Ruby Mountains. Start out in the parking lot and look ahead—you're going up and over the crest in front of you. Begin meandering up the hill and switchback right, where you'll soon cross through a cattle guard. It flattens out for a little bit. Enjoy every second here as it

Smith Lake sits at 9000 feet in the East Humboldt Wilderness →

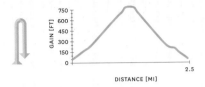

GAIN [FT]

750
600
450
300
150
0

2.5

DISTANCE [MI]

Lake Road for 11.5 miles until it ends at Angel Lake Campground. Note that this road closes in the winter, sometimes in October, so always call or check online before heading out! Also drive carefully; it's a beautiful route but has some steep drop-offs without guardrails.

**Google Maps:** bit.ly/timbersmithlake

**RESTROOMS** Yes

**FEE** None

**TREAT YOURSELF** Try one of the tens of flavors of Italian sodas at Bella's Restaurant & Espresso, 12 miles north in Wells.

Humboldt-Toiyabe National Forest
(775) 331-6444
Facebook @HumboldtToiyabeNF

**LENGTH** 2.5 miles out and back

**ELEVATION GAIN** 790 ft.

**HIKE + EXPLORE** 3 hours

**DIFFICULTY** Challenging—a steady uphill with some steep inclines and open exposure at altitude

**SEASON** Generally open July to October as weather and conditions allow.

**GET THERE** From Wells, take Humboldt Avenue south and turn right on NV-231/Angel

will continue to climb most of the rest of the way! Soon you'll reach a small sign that says "Smith" pointing to the left. Before you turn, take a look at the town of Wells and notice how small it looks from up here. You'll continue steadily heading up, passing through a tree alley. Power up here and catch your breath. Keep going up, up, and continue to work your way right, and soon you'll reach a small piney forest. There's one final push up to a bowl, and Smith Lake will be to your left. Power up here with lunch, gazing up at Greys Peak behind it and looking for trout inside of it, and head back the way you came. Consider camping right at beautiful Angel Lake when you're done.

# SCAVENGER HUNT

### Chimney Rock

You're near the oldest rocks in Nevada, the gneiss complex of Angel Lake. Can you make out the chimney spire? Sketch what you see in your nature journal, and imagine what you might see if someday you climbed all the way to the top.

The range around you was shaped by glaciers

### Black-billed magpie

It's hard to miss this flash of black and white whizzing past you in the sky, with a long green tail trailing behind. Anywhere on the ridge is a perfect place to stop, wait, and look for black-billed magpies—they love to sit on tops of trees and sing loudly. Take the magpie challenge: Sit quietly for 5 minutes while looking out over the horizon, and become a true wildlife watcher. Note every species you see in your nature journal.

*Pica hudsonia*

### Soap bush

Look for the beautiful purple flowers on this shrub in the springtime. If you combine the leaves with water, you can make soap like the Americans Indians did. For now, take a whiff and think if you'd like to smell like *Ceanothus* after your shower. It's also known as wild lilac.

*Ceanothus* sp.

### Pika

*Squeak! Squeak!* What's that noise? A mouse? Nope. These are pikas, the tailless rock-loving mammals who dwell in the alpine talus slopes of the pine forest near Smith Lake. They like high elevations. How about you? You're up pretty high today. Are you feeling out of breath?

*Ochotona princeps*

# 45

# TIME TRAVEL WITH GRIFFITH CANYON PETROGLYPHS

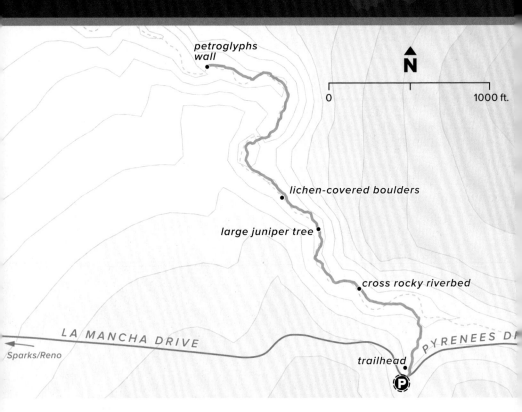

## YOUR ADVENTURE

Adventurers, today you're on the historical homelands of the Washoe at the base of the Pah Rah Mountain Range. The trail starts on the left side of the dirt road and is on private land. There isn't a sign for the trailhead, but as you hike down into the canyon you will see the trail take form. Continue toward the left side of the canyon. As you get lower you will come across

The petroglyphs in Griffith Canyon were carved about 1000 years ago →

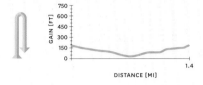

**LENGTH** 1.4 miles out and back

**ELEVATION GAIN** 164 ft.

**HIKE + EXPLORE** 2 hours

**DIFFICULTY** Moderate—the trail is rocky, but not too much elevation gain

**SEASON** Year-round. Hot in the summer; go in the early morning or evening so the canyon will create shade. Can get muddy/slippery after rains and in the springtime.

**GET THERE** From NV-445N, turn right on Calle de la Plata. Then turn right on to Valle Verde, turn right on Agua Fria Drive, turn left on El Molino Drive, and turn right on La Mancha Drive. After 1.2 miles, keep right to stay on La Mancha Drive. Continue straight onto Pyrenees Drive. After 0.8 mile, there will be a widened dirt area on the right of the hairpin turn for you to park. The trail starts across the road. The last 1.5 miles is a dirt road.

Google Maps: bit.ly/timbergriffithpetroglyphs

**RESTROOMS** No

**FEE** None

**TREAT YOURSELF** If you're driving back toward Reno, stop by Squeeze In for a yummy brunch, just 10 miles south of the trailhead.

BLM Carson City Field Office
775-885-6000

a few juniper trees, then reach a very large juniper tree right in the middle of the trail—a great spot to power up. The trail will eventually mesh with the riverbed rock, and you just continue following the wash. As the canyon starts to narrow, you'll come upon a large slab of rock on your right with the petroglyphs. Look around, as a few other rocks have petroglyphs as well. Remember to just take pictures, and don't scratch or write on the rocks. When you're done, follow your footsteps back.

# SCAVENGER HUNT

### Juniper

It may be surprising to see these evergreen (keep their leaves) trees in a barren canyon, but junipers are very drought resistant. Their roots grow deep and can find water far underground. American Indians have made medicine from the leaves to help treat vomiting, arthritis, and coughing. Look at their scaly needles. What do they smell like to you?

*Juniperus* sp.

### Rubber rabbitbrush

This is in the same family as sagebrush. American Indians have used it as a yellow dye, to make medicinal tea, and for chewing gum. Does this bush look like something you would want to chew on? It's also a great home for birds to nest in and other small animals seeking cover from raptors flying overhead. Could you hide from a raptor behind it?

*Ericameria nauseosa*

### Petroglyphs

Petroglyphs are carvings in the rocks, and these are some of the oldest ever found, 10,000-15,000 years ago. It's fun to imagine what the carvers' lives were like and what the pictures might mean. Do you see anything on the wall that looks recognizable?

Petroglyph wall

### Gold dust lichen

This yellow splatter on the rock usually grows on trees. It looks like someone spilled paint, but it's actually a living thing—a partnership between a fungus and an alga. Gold dust lichen thrives best in clean air because it absorbs nutrients and water directly from the air. Try to sketch its pattern in your nature journal.

*Chrysothrix candelaris*

### Big sagebrush

While sagebrush might seem like a boring plant because it's so common, it's actually very important to desert life. It's a good food source for mule deer, bighorn sheep, and jackrabbits. There are also almost 100 species of birds that nest or rest in sagebrush. It also creates an environment for the grass to grow. Rub some on your wrist for a little cologne like the cowboys used to do!

*Artemisia tridentata* ("three-toothed" in Latin)

# 46

# WILDLIFE WATCH AROUND SPOONER LAKE

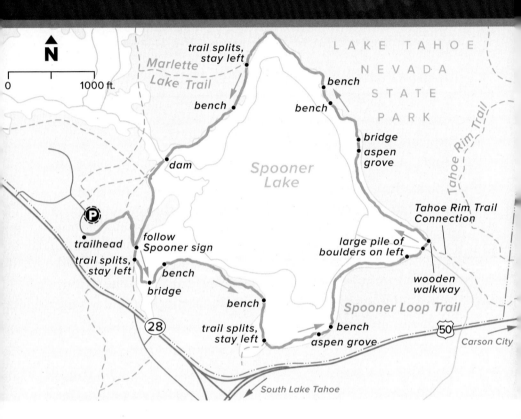

**N**

0    1000 ft.

*Marlette Lake Trail*

trail splits, stay left

bench

dam

*Spooner Lake*

LAKE TAHOE

NEVADA

STATE

PARK

bench

bench

bridge

aspen grove

*Tahoe Rim Trail*

Tahoe Rim Trail Connection

P

trailhead

follow Spooner sign

trail splits, stay left

bench

bridge

bench

large pile of boulders on left

wooden walkway

*Spooner Loop Trail*

28

trail splits, stay left

bench

aspen grove

50

*Carson City*

*South Lake Tahoe*

## YOUR ADVENTURE

Adventurers, today you're on the historical homelands of the Washoe nestled in the Lake Tahoe Basin. Follow the signs from the parking lot down to the trail that loops around the lake. You'll start on a dirt road going counterclockwise and turning right on the trail and soon come to a sign directing you to the trail to the left down lower to the lake. Cross a bridge,

**Spooner Lake is a man-made lake created by diverting water from nearby Marlette Lake** →

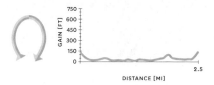

GAIN [FT] / DISTANCE [MI]

**LENGTH** 2.5-mile loop

**ELEVATION GAIN** 135 ft.

**HIKE + EXPLORE** 2 hours

**DIFFICULTY** Easy—the trail is easy to follow and has little elevation gain, but can be long for little legs

**SEASON** Year-round. Is covered in snow November–April, and you'll need proper footwear (snowshoes or spikes). Spring

has wonderful waterfowl and wildflowers, and the aspen turn bright yellow in fall.

**GET THERE** Follow US-50W from Carson City for 10 miles. Turn right onto NV-28S. After 0.7 mile, turn into the parking area marked for Spooner Lake.

Google Maps: bit.ly/timberspoonerlake

**RESTROOMS** Yes

**FEE** $5 ($10 for out-of-state plates)

**TREAT YOURSELF** Stop by The Baked Bear, 13 miles south in South Lake Tahoe, and try one of their famous ice cream sandwiches.

Lake Tahoe Nevada State Park
(775) 831-0494
Facebook @SandHarborOfficial

pass a couple of benches, and arrive at a trail split. Stay left here. You'll walk around a meadow where there are signs alerting you to stay on the trail, as it is a nesting area. Do you see any birds building their nests? Cross a wooden bridge and soon you'll be at another trail junction with the Tahoe Rim Trail; stay left here, following the signs for Spooner Lake, named after Michele Spooner, an entrepreneur in the logging and mining industry. As you make your way around the lake, you'll be surrounded by ponderosa pines, aspens, and lots of other plants and pass a few more benches and bridge. Reach another junction with the Marlette Lake Trail; stay straight here. Pass another bench, small dam, and bathroom, and you'll be back at the junction where you started. Turn left back to the parking lot. Consider renting a cabin or staying up at North Canyon Campground up the road.

# SCAVENGER HUNT

### Mountain chickadee

Spooner Lake is a great spot for bird-watching. This songbird can be seen flitting through the high branches of the trees. You may even spot one hang-

ing upside down as it picks insects and seeds from the pine cones! These birds are prepared and like to stash away food for when the weather makes food hard to come by. They are very vocal and even have a song that sounds like their name: *chick-a-dee, chick-a-dee*! Do your best *chick-a-dee* song and see if they hear you.

*Poecile gambeli* (*Poecile* is derived from the Greek word for "colorful")

### Osprey

If you notice a large bird of prey with a white underbelly, it's probably an osprey. These raptors mostly eat fish and love to catch them at Spooner Lake. When an osprey spots a fish as it flies above the lake, it dives headfirst at up to 80 miles per hour! At the last moment, it turns to go in with its feet and sharp talons extended to spear the fish. Often, the fish can be as big as the bird is!

*Pandion haliaetus*

### Brown's peony

Search for these intricate flowers on the south side of the lake in the aspen groves. These bloom from April to June. The flowers can be a little hard to

spot because they hang down low to the ground. Look closely at its maroon petals with yellow tips and bright yellow stamens (the part that fertilizes a flower). Try to draw and color them in your nature journal. The Washoe people made a medicine with the roots to treat lung ailments.

*Paeonia brownii*

### Grinding stone

On the north side of the lake, just off the trail and closer to the lake, you might spot a rock with perfectly round circles carved in it. These are mortars. The Washoe people who used to pass through this area would use smaller rocks to grind foods like acorns, pine nuts, and other seeds in mortars like this one. When you get home, ask your lead hikers if you can grind some spices together on something hard at your house.

Grinding stone near the lake

# 47

# INVESTIGATE THE RUINS AT FORT CHURCHILL

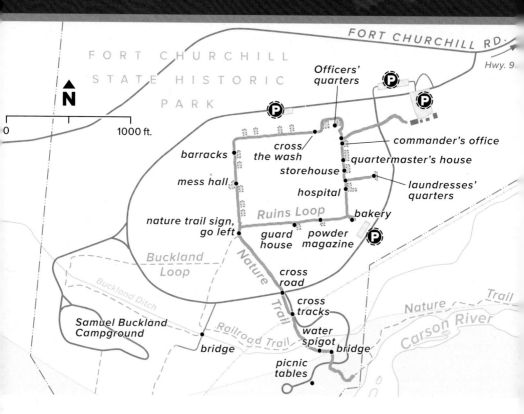

## YOUR ADVENTURE

Adventurers, today you're on the historical homelands of the Northern Paiute, Washoe, and Western Shoshone. Just to the right of the museum is a sign where the trail starts. Hike down on the dirt path lined with rocks, cross the street, and you'll be at the start of the Ruins Loop—you'll go counter-clockwise and turn right for this one. Take your time looking at the old

The path circles around the ruins at Fort Churchill →

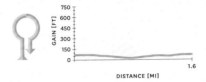

GAIN [FT]

750
600
450
300
150
0

1.6

DISTANCE [MI]

**LENGTH** 1.6-mile lollipop loop

**ELEVATION GAIN** 72 ft.

**HIKE + EXPLORE** 2 hours

**DIFFICULTY** Easy—not much elevation gain but hike can feel long for littles

**SEASON** Year-round. Exercise caution in the summer, as it lacks any shade and rattlesnake sightings are more common. Fall brings comfortable temperatures, lighting is ideal for photography, and the cottonwood trees along the Carson River are changing color.

**GET THERE** From Carson City, follow the US-50 east for 30 miles. Turn right onto Ramsey Weeks Cutoff. After 3.4 miles, turn right onto US-95 and drive for 4 miles. Then turn right onto Fort Churchill Road. After the pay station, the museum and trailhead are on the left.

Google Maps: bit.ly/timberfortchurchill

**RESTROOMS** Yes

**FEE** $5 ($10 for out-of-state plates)

**TREAT YOURSELF** Make a stop 24 miles north in Fernley at the Black Bear Diner and get yourself a slice of chocolate or banana cream pie.

Fort Churchill State Historic Park
(775) 577-2345
Facebook @FortChurchillStateHistoricPark

buildings that used to be a barracks, mess hall, hospital, and more. Stick to the trail and don't go inside these old buildings. Around the loop, take the Nature Trail to the left and you'll cross the road and a train track. This is an operational railroad track, so make sure a train isn't coming! Soon, you will be in the shade of the cottonwood trees. There are picnic tables off to the right to enjoy your lunch or snack here. Power up and follow your steps back to finish the loop trail. Visit the museum and consider camping at the Samuel Bucklands Campground just down the road.

# SCAVENGER HUNT

### Saltlover

This plant, as you might guess from the name, thrives in locations where the salt content in the soil is very high. It sits low with its branches stretching out like an octopus. Look for its clustered flowers in the late spring and summer and its tiny fruit. Can you count how many tiny flowers are on one stalk?

*Halogeton glomeratus* (*hal* means "salt" in Greek)

### Russian thistle tumbleweed

Though you're probably more likely to see a dried-up tumbleweed rolling across the desert than a live one, it does start off as a plant in the ground just like any other. At the end of the summer, Russian thistle plants detach from their roots and begin their tumbling journey to spread thousands of seeds for miles. Can you do a somersault? Find a safe, fairly clean space and give your best tumble on the trail.

*Salsola tragus*

## Great Basin rattlesnake

These reptiles like living in the desert because it is dry and warm. They are cold-blooded and rely on an external heat source, like the sun, to warm their bodies. If it gets too hot, they will retreat to the shade or underground so they don't overheat. Did you know their rattles are made of keratin—the same thing your fingernails and hair are? Rattlesnakes would rather retreat than strike, but if you see one don't bother it. How do you keep people away from you when you don't want to be bothered?

*Crotalus lutosus* (*Crotalus* is derived from the Greek word for "rattle")

## Buildings

Fort Churchill was built in 1860 to provide protection for early settlers in mining towns. The soldiers stationed at Fort Churchill provided protection for the area's wagon roads, the California Trail, and the riders of the Pony Express. The Pony Express was a service like today's post office—it delivered mail. Men would ride horses from station to station, passing the mail they carried along the way. Fort Churchill was abandoned in 1869. While you're walking around these old ruins, take time to imagine what this street looked like when it was busy.

The barracks at Fort Churchill; an 1862 drawing by Grafton Tyler Brown

# 48

# HIKE NEAR LAKE TAHOE TO MONKEY ROCK

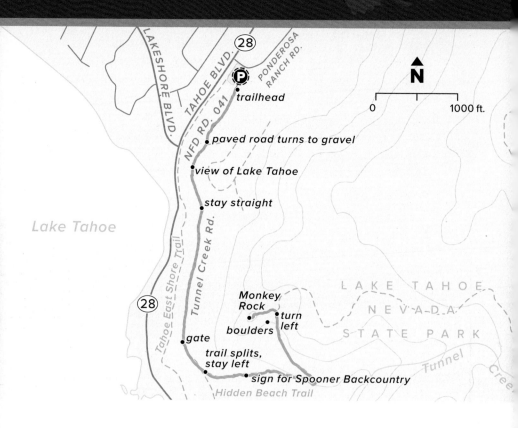

## YOUR ADVENTURE

Adventurers, today you're on the historical homelands of the Washoe. The trail starts on a paved road. Walk uphill until you reach the dirt path. Here the trail levels out and you'll have a gorgeous view of Lake Tahoe to your right. Eventually you'll come to a gate where you pay the $2 per hiker fee (cash only) for entering the Spooner Backcountry. From here the trail starts

Monkey Rock sits on the ridge above Lake Tahoe →

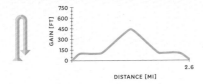

**LENGTH** 2.6 miles out and back

**ELEVATION GAIN** 456 ft.

**HIKE + EXPLORE** 2 hours

**DIFFICULTY** Challenging—this trail has strong elevation gain

**SEASON** Year-round. In winter will need proper footwear (snowshoes or spikes).

**GET THERE** From Carson City, follow US-50 for 10 miles. Turn right onto NV-28S and drive for 10 miles, then turn right onto Ponderosa Ranch Road and park near the Tunnel Creek Cafe.

Google Maps: bit.ly/timbermonkeyrock

**RESTROOMS** Yes

**FEE** Hourly rate varies depending on time of year and time of day, ranging from $1 to $7 an hour on peak hours and holidays

**TREAT YOURSELF** Right at the trailhead is Tunnel Creek Cafe, with lots of healthy options to refuel, including delicious smoothies.

Lake Tahoe–Nevada State Park
(775) 831-0494
Facebook @Lake Tahoe State Park Nevada

to gain some elevation, curving up to the left as you hike up to your destination. You'll pass signs for other trails, but keep hiking on the main trail until you reach a turnoff to the left where there are large boulders and a wooden beam you walk over—it's not marked, so keep an eye on your mileage and map. There is one last steep push to the top, where you'll find a large pile of very large boulders. See if you can spot the Reclining Rock Chair. Walk on the right side of the pile and off to your right to see Monkey Rock. Take time to enjoy the panoramic view of Lake Tahoe as well. When you're done enjoying the view, follow the trail back to your car.

# SCAVENGER HUNT

### Jeffrey pine

These evergreen (keep their leaves) trees are the most common tree around Lake Tahoe. Put your nose up to one of them and take a big whiff. What do you smell? Some people say they smell like vanilla, lemon, apple, or even butterscotch. Its bark has big scaly brown pieces. Take a piece of paper from your nature journal and a pencil; do a bark rubbing to see what it looks like.

*Pinus jeffreyi*

### Monkey Rock

Granite is a metamorphic rock that is made from cooled magma (lava) underneath the Earth's surface. This might just be Lake Tahoe's most famous rock. No one knows for sure why it looks like a monkey, but there's a rumor that years ago a local came up and carved it to look more monkey-like than it already did. Do you see a monkey shape or something else?

This granite rock is shaped like a monkey.

### Steller's jay

This blue bird with a fun black mohawk is loud and proud. Steller's jays like to eat insects, seeds, berries, nuts, and even small animals. They can

fly, but like to hop around on the ground and in the branches, pausing to take in their surroundings. These stops can give you time to get a good look and maybe even try to get a photo. Listen for their *shook-shook-shook-shook* call.

*Cyanocitta stelleri*

### Lake Tahoe

One of the best parts of this hike is the incredible view you get of Lake Tahoe. It's more than 2 million years old and the second deepest lake in the country! It's 1645 feet deep, which is deeper than the Empire State Building is tall. It's such a cool spot that it gets 15 million people visiting it every year, including you!

A stunning view of Lake Tahoe

### Bush chinquapin

While you're walking along the trail, you'll notice a lot of shrubs. Look out for this one—it has an interesting surprise. This is an evergreen plant that grows a spiny nut that squirrels and chipmunks love to eat. They grow and drop in the fall. Collect as many as possible in 1 minute, like a squirrel might.

*Chrysolepis sempervirens*

# 49

# EXPLORE THE GHOST TOWN OF RHYOLITE

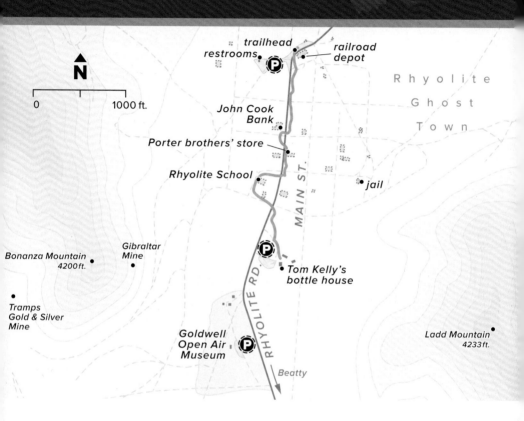

## YOUR ADVENTURE

Adventurers, today you're on the historical homelands of the Western Shoshone and exploring one of about 600 ghost towns in Nevada. You'll begin at the Rhyolite train depot across the street from the parking lot and restroom. Explore the old train depot and the Union Pacific train caboose behind it, then walk carefully along Rhyolite Road. You'll come to the

You'll explore the ruins of Rhyolite, a former mining town that was once home to 6000 people →

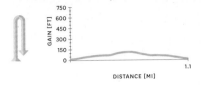

**LENGTH** 1.1 miles out and back

**ELEVATION GAIN** 118 ft.

**HIKE + EXPLORE** 2 hours

**DIFFICULTY** Easy—fairly flat and partially on pavement and dirt road; be very careful for cars

**SEASON** Year-round. Summer is extremely hot and the trail is fully exposed, so explore in the early morning hours. Spring, fall, and winter are good times to visit for cooler temperatures.

**GET THERE** From Beatty, take Highway 374 south for 4 miles. Turn right on Rhyolite Road and drive 1.2 miles. You'll begin at the Rhyolite labyrinth parking lot on the left.

Google Maps: bit.ly/timberrhyolite

**RESTROOMS** No

**FEE** None

**TREAT YOURSELF** Mel's Diner in Beatty has a fun atmosphere and breakfast and lunch items like burgers and shakes.

BLM Tonopah Field Office
(775) 482-7800

three-story John Cook Bank Building on your right. Explore around the building and continue south to the Porter brothers' storefront on the left. Next are the Rhyolite School ruins on your right and then Tom Kelly's bottle house. You can head back or continue to the Goldwell Open Air Museum with cool outdoor sculptures. Return the way you came.

# SCAVENGER HUNT

### John Cook Bank Building

Ghost towns are areas that once were popular but went bust once the town's main industry, like mining, stopped producing jobs. When gold was found in this area in 1904, the town of Rhyolite began to spring up around the mining camps. This bank cost over $90,000 to build, which is equivalent to $2.5 million today! Inside there were Italian marble

floors, mahogany woodwork, electric lights, telephones, and indoor plumbing. In 1910 it was the last business to close in Rhyolite. Sketch what you think it looked like.

The Cook Bank Building as it looked in the center of town ... and today

### Bottle house

Tom T. Kelly, a miner, built his house in 1906, using 50,000 beer and liquor bottles. He collected all of them from 50 local saloons in just 6 months! What recycled material would you build with?

Adobe mud is holding the bottles together

### School ruins

Does this look like your school? Imagine 250 schoolchildren coming here every day. Soon after it was built, the mines began to close and local banks failed. The building's lights and power were finally turned off in 1916 as families and students moved out of town.

The Rhyolite School was built in 1909

### HD & LD Porter Store

This store opened in 1902 and closed in 1910. It sold mining supplies and food for the miners who lived here. The Porter brothers also had stores nearby in Ballarat, Beatty, and Pioneer. Would you rather have been a miner or a business owner that sold things to miners?

The Porter brothers' Store

### Rhyolite train depot

The Las Vegas & Tonopah Railroad started running trains to Rhyolite in 1906, when this Spanish-style depot was built at a cost of $130,000. The

depot closed in 1914. In the 1930s, it became a casino and bar, and later it became a small museum and souvenir shop that stayed open into the 1970s. Sketch the building in your nature journal and think how the elements of it look different from today's buildings.

The Spanish-style train depot

# 50

# MUST-SEE MARY JANE FALLS

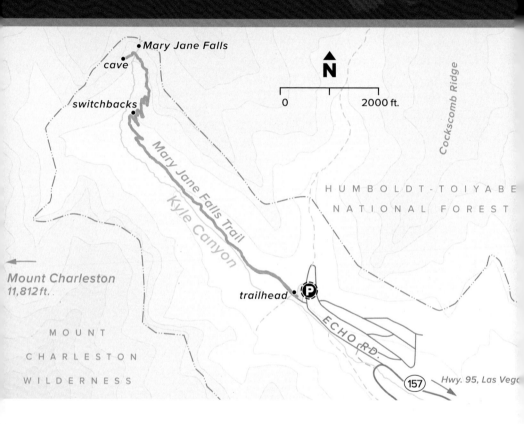

## YOUR ADVENTURE

Adventurers, today you're on the historical homelands of the Chemehuevi and exploring the Kyle Canyon area of the Humboldt-Toiyabe National Forest. You'll begin by heading straight up the side of Kyle Canyon—the incline continues the whole way, so take power-up stops whenever you need to. Be on the lookout after 0.7 mile for the switchbacks to begin,

**A beautiful seasonal waterfall awaits you in the mountains west of Las Vegas →**

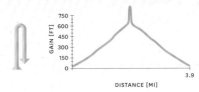

GAIN [FT]
750
600
450
300
150
0

3.9

DISTANCE [MI]

**LENGTH** 3.9 miles out and back

**ELEVATION GAIN** 1135 ft.

**HIKE + EXPLORE** 3 hours

**DIFFICULTY** Challenging—rocky, long, and lots of elevation gain at high elevation, but a perfect challenge for older or more seasoned little hikers; be sure to acclimate, drink plenty of water, and turn around if you get nauseous or have a headache

**SEASON** Spring, summer, and fall. Parking lot is closed in winter season with snow; spring offers peak water flow.

**GET THERE** From Las Vegas, take US-95 north to the US-157/Kyle Canyon Road exit and take that highway for 16.4 miles. At the traffic circle, take the second exit for US-157 and continue for 4 miles. At the hairpin turn, continue straight onto Echo Road and go until the road ends at the parking lot.

Google Maps: bit.ly/timbermaryjane

**RESTROOMS** Yes

**FEE** None

**TREAT YOURSELF** Great donuts and more await at Blooming Buns Bakehouse just 24 miles east toward Las Vegas.

Humboldt-Toiyabe National Forest
Spring Mountains National Recreation Area
(702) 872-5486

with a log blocking the trail continuing straight. The rocks get a little looser on this mile-long series of switchbacks. Soon the waterfall appears, dropping over a sheer rockface. Cool off here, and if you've got more energy, you can continue on a bit further to explore a neat cave. Head back the way you came and consider a night under the stars just down the road at Fletcher View Campground.

# SCAVENGER HUNT

### White fir

Look for the pretty blue-green needles of this evergreen (doesn't lose its leaves) tree sticking straight up. Crush a fallen needle. Do you smell a lemon scent? Rub a little on your wrist for some tree-scented cologne.

*Abies concolor* ("of the same color" in Latin)

### Quaking aspen

This deciduous tree lights up the trail in the fall with beautiful yellows. Watch closely when the wind blows as the leaves quake in the wind—they almost look like a beautiful wind chime! Collect a few fallen leaves and make a beautiful wind chime of your own by stringing them together when you get home.

*Populus tremuloides* (derived from the Latin word for "trembling")

### Curl-leaf mountain mahogany

This twisty deciduous (loses its leaves) tree is easy to tell apart from the aspens and white firs on this trek. Look closely at its leathery leaves that curl toward the sun. Be sure to look for its yellow flowers in the spring and later its seeds, which sprout into long feathers.

*Cercocarpus ledifolius*

### Mount Charleston

Mount Charleston is the highest peak in the Spring Mountains, Nevada, rising up to an elevation of 11,916 feet. In the local Southern Paiute language, the mountain is known as Nuvagantu, which translates to "where snow sits" because snow is on the peak for half of the year and is visible from Las Vegas. What would you call this peak?

Mount Charleston, the peak is known as a sky island because of how far up it juts from the desert floor

# ACKNOWLEDGMENTS

There is nothing more reaffirming that we live in a world full of caring people than when hardworking rangers, parents, conservationists, biologists, geologists, and hikers call us back or respond to our emails, helping us get that species identification just right or verify the year a major discovery happened on the trail. Special thanks to rangers and outreach specialists of the parks Kevin Abel, Chelsea Phillipe, Trish Ackley, J. C. Ballard, Amanda Rowland, Kate Sorom, Kristin Sanderson, Amanda White, David Hercher, Jonathan Shafer, James Wells, Jared Rozich, Ranger Matt at Natural Bridges, Rachel Wootten, Austin Tumas, and Steve Micklus.

Grandparents are great hike leaders, too!

Huge thanks to Stacee Lawrence, Sarah Milhollin, Sarah Crumb, Cobi Lawson, Mike Dempsey, Melina Dorrance, Kathryn Juergens, Matt Burnett, Andrew Beckman, Lisa Brousseau, and the entire Timber Press family for believing in expanding to co-authors to reach even more states faster!

To Wendy's family—to Gail, Xavier, and Jaedon Moore for being her trusty guinea pigs; to her father, Alan, for being an amazing driver and hiker; to her husband, Garrison, for being head GPS tracker and cheerleader and chef; and to her mother, Ginny, for her research skills and always reminding us to top up the gas on rural roads; and to Larry for his impeccable windshield cleaning skills. This book is about family, and having a strong family supporting you makes adventure possible.

And to Hailey's family—to her husband, Logan, for being her biggest supporter; to her mom, Jo, for being her biggest inspiration and for joining her on some of these hikes (and carrying her toddler); to her dad, Dennis, for encouraging and raising her to know she could do big things; and to her friends for watching her toddler when she needed to do some kid-free hikes. And thank you to all of you for reading this and getting outside with each other! We can't wait to see the adventures you go on.

# PHOTO AND ILLUSTRATION CREDITS

*All photos are by the authors with the exception of those listed below.*

Bureau of Land Management, Nevada; p. 220 (bottom)

David Tarailo, Geoscientist-in-the Park, sponsored by the Geological Society of America, GeoCorps Program, 2012; p. 194 (top)

Glen S. Hopkinson, "Hole in the Rock." p. 147 (bottom)

Grafton Tyler Brown, 1862; public domain; p. 249 (middle, lithography)

Ted Muller, p. 235

Courtesy of Zion National Park Museum and Archives, ZION 2393, Historic Photograph Collection; p. 199 (bottom)

**Bug Guide**
Christopher Christie, p. 175 (bottom, right)

**Dreamstime**
Aaron Hinckley, p. 118 (top)

Alexneumayer, p. 209 (top)

Aliaksandr Nikitsin, p. 147 (top)

Alluring Nature; pp. 81, 83 (middle); 93

Alysta, p. 85

Amadeustx; pp. 173, 175 (top)

Andreistanescu, p. 131 (top)

Anton Foltin, p. 145

Aquamarine4; pp. 162 (top), 253 (top)

Bakusova, p. 221 (middle)

Brian Lasenby; pp. 67 (bottom), 237 (bottom)

Chon Kit Leong, p. 233 (middle)

Chris Curtis; pp. 103 (middle), 149, 179 (top), 191 (top)

Cjchiker, p. 75 (bottom)

Clifton Smith, p. 78 (top)

Cynthia Mccrary; pp. 126 (top), 147 (third), 154 (top)

Dana Kenneth Johnson, p. 99 (middle)

Daniel Larson; pp. 165, 166 (top)

David Burke, p. 182 (top)

Alan Cressler, p. 134 (bottom)
Andrey Zharkikh, p. 135 (middle)
Courtesy of Bat Conservation
   International and Minden
   Pictures/Michael Durham/
   the Bureau of Land
   Management; p. 216 (bottom)
Kai Larson, p. 185
NPS/Peri Sasnett, p. 208 (top)
Richard O'Neill, p. 233 (top)

**iStock**
Marieke Peche, p. 127 (top)

**Shutterstock**
Damiano Buffo, p. 255
Danita Delimont, p. 171 (top)
motive56, p. 257 (middle)
Ryan McGurl, p. 225 (middle)
vagabond54, p. 122 (bottom)

**Wikimedia**
Brewbooks, p. 107 (middle)
Colton, G. W., Colton's Atlas of the
   World Illustrating Physical and
   Political Geography, Vol 1, New
   York, 1855 (First Edition); p. 43
Connor Long, p. 187 (middle)
Eric in SF, p. 217 (top)
G. Thomas, p. 236 (top)
Georgialh, p. 233 (bottom)
Heather Kyoht Luterman,
   p. 102 (top, left)

James St. John, p. 195
   (middle, inset)
Jhodlof, p. 252 (top)
Jim Morefield, pp. 198 (top, left),
   229 (top)
Kenraiz; pp. 90 (bottom),
   130 (top, and inset)
Krzysztof Ziarnek, Kenraiz;
   p. 126 (bottom)
Morgan Hansen; p. 301 (top)
Randy C. Bunney, Great Circle
   Photographics, p. 280 (bottom)
Ron Knight, p. 244
VJAnderson, p. 225 (bottom)
Walter Siegmund, p. 90 (bottom)
Zion National Park, p. 66 (top)

Maps by Nick Trotter
Illustrations by Always with Honor

# INDEX

# ABOUT YOUR LEAD ADVENTURERS

**WENDY GORTON** holds a master's degree in learning technologies and is a former classroom teacher who grew up exploring Utah's canyons with her family. As part of her quest to bring science education alive, she worked as a National Geographic Fellow in Australia researching Tasmanian devils, a PolarTREC teacher-researcher in archaeology in Alaska, an Earthwatch teaching fellow in the Bahamas and New Orleans, and a GoNorth! teacher-explorer studying climate change via dogsled in Finland, Norway, and Sweden. Today, she is a global education consultant who has traveled to more than fifty countries to design programs, build communities, and inspire other educators to do the same. She enjoys mountain biking, rock climbing, kayaking, backpacking, yoga, photography, traveling, writing, and hanging out with her family and nephews. Follow her on social media @50hikeswithkids and email wendy@50hikeswithkids.com.

**HAILEY TERRY** has a bachelor's degree in public health. She is an avid hiker, backpacker, and rock climber and loves anything that gets her outside. She's a mother to two kids and loves bringing them along on all of her adventures. When her husband was deployed a few weeks after their first baby was born, she started sharing her experiences hiking solo with her baby as a new mom on Instagram @haileyoutside. Now she helps parents all over the world get outside with their kids, sharing her best tips for hiking in all seasons, backpacking, camping, and more. She has written a Hiking with Babies Guide, where she shares everything from how to dress your baby, dealing with naps, breastfeeding on the trail, and gear recommendations. She also has a blog, HaileyOutside.com, where you can read more detailed posts about getting outside with kids and sign up for her emails.